DORLING KINDERSLEY DK EYEWITNESS BOOKS

TECHNOLOGY

Glass-reinforced
plastic chair
(1960s)

Machine for testing
the hardness
of metals

Cyclonic-action
vacuum cleaner
(1993)

Food mixer (1992)

Monocoque bicycle (1992)

Record player (1920s)

Ring-pull on aluminum can lid

Aluminum

DK EYEWITNESS BOOKS

TECHNOLOGY

Written by
ROGER BRIDGMAN

Cellular telephone (1993)

Toy water pump made
from recycled materials

Computer simulation
of fan blade at takeoff

Theodolite
(18th century)

Dorling Kindersley

Making a coil pot

Micrometer

Miniature tube (1940)

Casting metal in a foundry

Dorling Kindersley
LONDON, NEW YORK, AUCKLAND, DELHI, JOHANNESBURG,
MUNICH, PARIS and SYDNEY

For a full catalog, visit
DK www.dk.com

Project editor Charyn Jones
Art editor Emma Boys
Designer Elaine C. Monaghan
Production Fiona Wright
Picture research Deborah Pownall
Managing editor Josephine Buchanan
Managing art editor Lynne Brown
Special photography Clive Streeter
Editorial consultant Eryl Davies
US editor Ray Rogers
US consultant Jefferey S. Kaufmann, PhD

This Eyewitness ® Book has been conceived by
Dorling Kindersley Limited and Editions Gallimard

Published in the United States by
DK Publishing, Inc.
375 Hudson Street
New York, New York 10014
6 8 10 9 7 5

Dorling Kindersley books are available at special discounts for bulk purchases
for sales promotions or premiums. Special editions, including personalized
covers, excerpts of existing guides, and corporate imprints can be created in
large quantities for specific needs. For more information, contact Special
Markets Dept., Dorling Kindersley Publishing, Inc., 95 Madison Ave.,
New York, NY 10016; Fax: (800) 600-9098

Library of Congress Cataloging-in-Publication Data
Bridgman, Roger.
Technology / written by Roger Bridgman.
p. cm. — (Eyewitness Books)
Includes index.
1. Technology—Juvenile literature. [1. Technology.]
I. Title. II. Series.
T48.B82 2000 600—dc20   94-34859
                                                  CIP
                                                  AC

ISBN 0-7894-6186-2 (pb)
ISBN 0-7894-4887-4 (hc)

Color reproduction by Colourscan, Singapore
Printed in China by Toppan Printing Co. (Shenzhen) Ltd.

Oil lamp

Photomicrograph of a seed

Testing a jet engine for noise

A load on a beam bridge

Contents

TIG welding

What is technology?

TECHNOLOGY IS THE SCIENCE AND ART of making and using things. Human beings are uniquely able to turn the materials of the natural world into tools and machines that can help them live. Although other animals can make things and use tools – the otter uses rocks to break open a shell – the way they do this hardly ever changes. Human technology is different: people are able to see new needs, find new ways of meeting them, and spot the value of accidental discoveries. The discovery of fire, for example, and its ability to transform clay into pottery or rocks into metals, made the modern world possible. Over the last few hundred years, scientists have found out why materials and machines behave the way they do. Using this knowledge, old materials have been improved, new materials invented, and science and mathematics brought to bear on products as different as swimwear and aircraft. Making things starts with design – working out what is needed and how to provide it. Designers (pp. 52-53) now have a vast range of materials, methods, and components with which to realize their ideas, and today much of their work can be done by computers. But producing something that works well, costs little, and appeals to its users remains a truly human art.

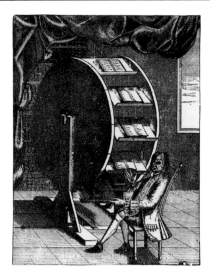

VICTORIAN READING WHEEL
The urge to invent is strong. This 19th-century gadget was an attempt to offer scholars of the pre-electronic age the sort of facilities we now get from a personal computer (p. 55). By turning the wheel, a wide range of literature could be accessed. But like so many would-be inventors, the reading wheel's unknown creator failed to consider cost and convenience.

CHINESE SHADOOF
People cannot live without a reliable supply of water for themselves, their crops, and their animals (pp. 44-45). Ingenious ways of tapping and distributing water (p. 22) allow life to go on in places that would otherwise be too dry. This simple cranelike device, the shadoof, has been used all over Asia for thousands of years. By adding a weight to the end of a pole, its clever, practical designer made it easy to lift buckets of river water into the irrigation channels that carry water to thirsty crops.

Weapons slung under wing

FLYING WITH STEAM
This 19th-century steam-powered flying machine shows no understanding of the lift needed to keep a man airborne, let alone the heavy steam engine strapped to his chest. And even if the would-be aviator had managed to take to the air, there is no way the contraption can be steered.

A CROSS-CHANNEL FLIGHT
Solving the problem of flight proved to be beyond the artist. It took science and mathematics to get aircraft off the ground. In 1909 Louis Blériot (1872-1936), a wealthy French manufacturer, built this fragile assembly of wood, wire, and canvas, *Blériot XI*, and flew from France to England. He won a prize of £1000 for the first powered flight to cross a sea.

Laminated wood propeller

Three-cylinder engine

Cotton covering

Pilot sits here

Fuselage is made of ash

Wires to control the wing warp

Wing made from cotton stretched over frame of ash and spruce

Diagonal bracing of piano wire

Rubber tires

Rudder helps control direction

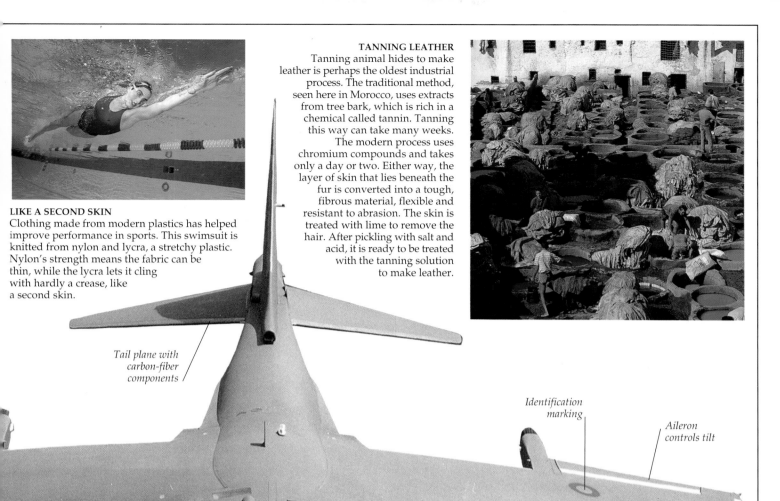

LIKE A SECOND SKIN
Clothing made from modern plastics has helped improve performance in sports. This swimsuit is knitted from nylon and lycra, a stretchy plastic. Nylon's strength means the fabric can be thin, while the lycra lets it cling with hardly a crease, like a second skin.

TANNING LEATHER
Tanning animal hides to make leather is perhaps the oldest industrial process. The traditional method, seen here in Morocco, uses extracts from tree bark, which is rich in a chemical called tannin. Tanning this way can take many weeks. The modern process uses chromium compounds and takes only a day or two. Either way, the layer of skin that lies beneath the fur is converted into a tough, fibrous material, flexible and resistant to abrasion. The skin is treated with lime to remove the hair. After pickling with salt and acid, it is ready to be treated with the tanning solution to make leather.

Tail plane with carbon-fiber components

Identification marking

Aileron controls tilt

Movable exhaust nozzle

Turbofan engine

Canopy of acrylic plastic (pp. 26-27)

Air intake

Pilot sits in ejector seat

MILITARY AIRCRAFT
The latest materials, skills, and ideas come together in the sleek shapes of modern aircraft. Like their canvas-covered ancestors, they fly by pushing their wings through the air at high speed. The shape of each wing causes a drop in the pressure of the air rushing over its top surface, and the air below pushes the wing upward, conquering gravity. But the British Aerospace Harrier, first flown in 1966, has one more way to fly. Its powerful jet engines (p. 36) can be made to direct their thrust downward, pushing the aircraft straight up from any convenient ship or tiny field before it speeds onward at up to 740 mph (1180 km/h).

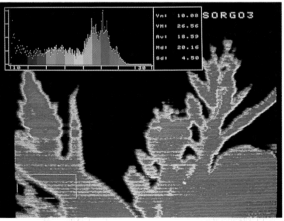

INCREASING SORGHUM YIELDS
Science and technology work together to tackle urgent problems, some of them brought about by technology itself. This picture uses infrared imaging (p. 59) to reveal the response of a cereal, sweet sorghum, to watering. The aim is to increase yields of the plant, which can be fermented to produce synfuels such as alcohol. These fuels may one day replace our rapidly shrinking stocks of oil.

Transforming materials

MANY THOUSANDS OF YEARS AGO, people began to find ways of changing the simple materials they found around them into more useful forms that could help them survive in a hostile world. Soft clay was available everywhere and easy to shape, but it was fragile. Transformed by fire, it became the hard, waterproof body of a cooking pot or storage jar. Even common sand can be transformed by heating it with other substances to make the smooth, transparent material called glass. Other rocks yield strong, tough metals when heated with the right materials. All of these processes require energy, often in the form of heat. And all of them are still in use today, although they now take place on a huge scale, using much more energy than in the past.

GRECIAN CRAFTS
The bottom of this ancient Greek cup was decorated by scraping away a black coating to reveal the red clay underneath. The craft worker is shown fashioning leather into sturdy sandals.

A COIL POT
Pots are made from fine white or red clay. The clay is washed to get rid of grit, then dried until it is pliable but not wet. Any air bubbles inside the clay would expand when the pots are fired, causing them to explode, so the clay is hammered or squeezed to force out trapped air. It is then ready for the potter.

The coils are used to build up the shape

1 MAKING THE SHAPE
Round pots are the strongest, and coiling is one way of making a round pot. The prepared clay is rolled out to make a long, thin "worm." This is then moistened with slip, a creamy mixture of clay and water.

The potter's hands smooth the surface

2 SMOOTHING THE SURFACE
The "hills" created by the coils of clay are flattened into the "valleys" between them using the hands or a special smoothing tool. After drying, the pot is fired by heating it to a high temperature in a special oven called a kiln.

The glaze is brushed onto the pot

Interesting effects are produced by varying the ingredients of the glaze

3 THE GLAZE
After 8-10 hours of firing, the clay has changed into a strong but porous material known as "biscuit." To make the pot useful, the surface must be glazed to coat it with a layer of glass. The glaze contains glass suspended in water, together with chemicals to provide color.

4 THE FINISHED POT
The pot is fired again, and the glaze turns into molten glass which coats the surface to produce beautiful effects.

The element cobalt in the glaze gives the blue color

A RAW EGG
Many natural products, like this egg, are made up mostly of proteins. Eggs have been used as a source of protein since prehistoric times – and not just for food. Because they are made of very large molecules, protein solutions like egg white are sticky and can be used as glues or binders for paints.

Viscous white of egg

COOKING TECHNOLOGY
Food, like everything else, is made up of tiny particles called atoms, joined together into molecules. Heat transforms materials by supplying the energy their molecules need to rearrange themselves into different molecules. Cooking breaks up large molecules into smaller ones that are easier to digest, and also creates new flavors and textures. The mixture in this machine is a greasy paste until the chemistry of cooking turns it into delicious biscuits.

A COOKED EGG
After heating in boiling water, the proteins in the egg white no longer form a clear solution. Their chemical structure has been broken down, making the egg easier to digest.

The egg white is no longer clear

Making glass bottles

Glass has been made for over 6,000 years. It is produced by heating sand with soda and limestone. Modern glasses contain other ingredients to improve color and to provide special properties such as heat resistance. Glass seems like a solid but is really a slow-moving liquid. If glass is made red-hot, it starts to flow more quickly and can be formed into complex shapes by blowing, molding, or a combination of the two. Glass is resistant to corrosion, making it useful for bottles and jars. Unfortunately, it is also brittle, so glass bottles have to be thick to survive everyday use. But where transparency and hardness are essential, such as in windows or camera lenses, glass has no equal.

Limestone

Sand

Soda

THE ESSENTIAL INGREDIENTS
Glass is made from widely available materials: sand, soda, and limestone. These ingredients combine together to produce an easily melted glass that is resistant to water.

Rod to hold the glass

MODEL BOTTLE
Bottles come in many shapes and sizes, each designed for a specific purpose. Shoppers will reject a bottle that looks wrong for the product it contains or appears to be too small. To see what a new bottle design will look like, glassware makers use model shapes, like this ketchup bottle carved from plastic, or computer imaging (p. 55).

(p. 55).

The ingredients for glass are heated in a furnace

VAT TO BOTTLE
Most bottles are blown from molten glass in a few seconds on large, automatic machines. Glass drops into an inverted mold and is forced upward by compressed air. After blowing, the bottles are cooled slowly to prevent uneven contraction that would stress the glass.

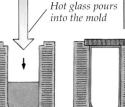

Hot glass pours into the mold

The parison is ready to be placed inside the mold

Glass is tapped on a flat plate to shape it

Stopper *Air pushes the glass against the mold*

MOLDING A BOTTLE
Bottles are shaped by air. To make a bottle by hand, a metal mold is locked around a bubble of molten glass called a parison. When the parison is inflated, the pressure of the air forces the glass into the shape of the mold. Most bottles are now made on automatic machinery, but the principle remains the same.

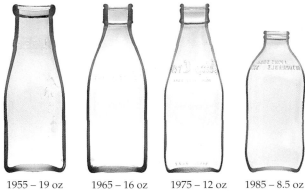

1955 – 19 oz   1965 – 16 oz   1975 – 12 oz   1985 – 8.5 oz

CHANGING BOTTLE SHAPES
These four bottles each hold the same amount of milk, yet the oldest weighs more than twice as much as the newest. By saving weight, improved designs reduce transportation costs for both suppliers and consumers.

Stone Age hand ax

Cutting materials

TECHNOLOGY REARRANGES THE WORLD to suit our needs. One important kind of rearrangement is separating things that are joined together, like a tree and its branches or an animal and its skin. This is usually done by cutting, in which intense local pressure is applied to overcome forces that hold materials together. For a given force, pressure increases as the area it acts on is reduced. A knife edge has a very small area, so is easily pushed through materials that could not easily be broken in any other way. Since the knife blade experiences the same pressure as whatever it cuts, it has to be made of stronger material. Some kinds of stone such as flint and obsidian (a natural glass) are strong enough to cut natural materials, and easily form sharp edges. The flint ax of 20,000 years ago (left) was split off a larger piece of flint by banging it with another stone, then carefully flaked around its edges to produce the finished blade. Flint tools like this were used for thousands of years. But metals make better tools, because they are tough (resistant to cracking) as well as strong (pp. 12-13). Knives and axes are not the only cutting and shaping tools. Others, such as scissors and shears, split material in a different way, by forcing neighboring regions to move in opposite directions.

STONE AGE AX
Technology started from the ground up. Before metals were discovered, people worked with what they found around them. For cutting and shaping, they used a glass-hard stone called flint. It flakes easily, naturally producing a sharp edge.

INGENIOUS SAWING MACHINE
A saw breaks the tough fibers of wood a few at a time and then scrapes away the loosened material to reach more. Sawing is slow, hard work; this ingenious 19th-century logging machine uses leg-power to speed up the process.

A CUTTING MACHINE
The lathe is one of the basic tools of engineering. It "turns" components to a circular cross-section by rotating them against a fixed cutter. This lathe is turning a brass component to a specified size. Tools of this kind, which are large and fixed in position, are called machine tools. They give much higher accuracy and output than is possible with hand tools. Modern automatic lathes churn out thousands of precision parts (p. 55) every hour under the control of computers.

Pipe for cooling fluid (turned off for clarity)

Headstock holds work steady

Chuck holds the work piece

Brass rod being turned

Cutting tool

CHAIN SAW VERSUS MUSCLE
Cutting and shaping have changed since ancient times. The power for tree felling and logging now comes from a gas-burning engine mounted on a chain saw, not from human muscle. The saw's cutting edge is made not from stone but from a special steel alloy (p. 14) that keeps its sharp edge as the work of cutting heats it up. Before such equipment was available, it could take several people many hours to fell a tall tree. Now the job is done in minutes.

WORKING WITH TIN

In spite of their strength, metals are quite easy to work by hand. Unlike wood, they have no grain, so they cut cleanly. They also hold their shape once they are bent. Thin steel works well, and its one great drawback, rust, can be overcome by coating the steel with a layer of tin to produce tinplate. Normally used for cans, tinplate is sometimes used by craftsmen to make simple domestic utensils. The pieces for the water dipper (p. 12) are cut out with tin snips, a tool like scissors but providing more leverage and so exerting greater force. Gentle hammering flattens out any distortion.

Base

Handle

Main body of the dipper

SHAPING WITH PLIERS

Metals have the useful property of distorting permanently under high stress without losing their strength. This tinsmith is bending the tinplate with pliers to shape it into a cookie cutter. The metal gets stiffer when it is bent, an effect known as "work hardening," and this helps the product keep its shape in use. This slow process demonstrates the ancient craft of the tinsmith and satisfies those who prefer handmade products.

The finished cookie cutter

Pliers are used to shape the cutter

MOROCCAN WOOD TURNING

This Moroccan craft worker is making decorative wooden parts from wood supported between two pivots and turned with a foot, leaving the hands free to manipulate the cutting tool. Slightly less primitive lathes, operated by a treadle pulling on a cord wrapped around the wood, have been in use for thousands of years. Modern lathes are precision instruments. They grip the work piece firmly in a rotating chuck, and also have the cutting tool mounted rigidly on a holder running in guides to give repeatable accuracy. However, this simple lathe produces turnings with a wayward charm all their own.

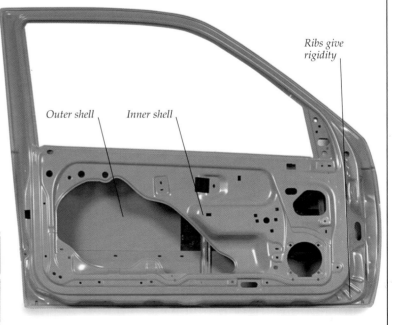

Jointed tube allows cooling fluid to be directed where it is needed

Tool holder

Bolt to secure tool holder

Slide way for tool holder to move along

Ribs give rigidity

Outer shell   *Inner shell*

SHAPING CARS

In car production (pp. 42-43) the same shape is needed over and over again, so tools are made that form components with just a few strokes. Sheet steel can be squeezed into shape between sculptured steel dies. If holes are needed – as here for the windows – they can be cut by a punch that fits closely inside a hole in the die. The punch forces the metal through the hole, shearing it at the edges. Paper punches use the same principle.

What are metals?

WITHOUT METALS, THE MODERN WORLD could not have been created. Metals offer a matchless blend of strength, toughness, and stiffness, but they are easy to cut and shape in many different ways. The use of metals revolutionized hunting and farming (pp. 44-45). Metals were essential to the transportation revolution that started with iron railroads and ships. Aerospace technology depends on light metals like titanium to provide great strength at high temperatures. And without the special electrical properties of metals, electric power, electronic communications, and computers could not have happened. Even the lightbulb relies on metallic technology: its tungsten metal filament can deliver a thousand hours of white-hot light without breaking.

Saxon spear
(AD 400-500)

METALS IN HISTORY
Native copper – small pieces of pure metal embedded in rocks – was probably the first metal to be used, around 8,000 years ago. Precious metals, like the gold from this Japanese mine, were treasured by the rich and powerful for their magical beauty.

DEADLY THROW
The art of the early blacksmith was to hammer iron into the right shape with the right proportion of impurities, producing a cutting tip that was hard (p. 15) and did not crack.

Zinc

Iron

Aluminum

VALUABLE METALS
It was not until the art of smelting by fire was discovered, about 6,000 years ago, that metals could be extracted from metal-rich rocks (ores) in worthwhile quantities. Iron is the most widely used metal, usually in the form of steel. Aluminum is the most abundant but needs expensive electricity to extract it from its ore. Copper was the first metal to be discovered and used. Zinc forms valuable alloys (p. 14). Lead is soft and pliable and does not corrode, while tin is often used as a thin coating on steel to make cans (p. 11).

Copper

Lead

Tinplate water dipper

BREAKING POINT
Although the wire from which this paper clip is made is thin, it is impossible to break it by hand with a straight pull. But bending it produces stresses that take the metal beyond the elastic region, in which it can spring back to shape, into the plastic region, where it is permanently distorted.

Clip is bent out of shape

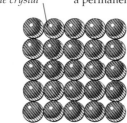

1 BENDING THE CLIP
If the steel clip is bent slightly out of shape, the atoms of the metal can snap back into place. But with greater stress applied, the atoms of the metal begin to slip over each other. They can no longer regain their original positions, and this causes a permanent change in shape.

The clip becomes brittle and snaps

2 BREAKING THE CLIP
Defects in the pattern of atoms in a metal, called dislocations (p. 15), allow the atoms to move and absorb the energy that bending feeds into the metal. Without dislocations the metal would be unable to distort without breaking. Continual changes of shape tangle the dislocations so they cannot move. The metal gets harder to bend and snaps.

17th-century
samurai sword

A perfect metal would have its atoms arranged in neat rows as a single crystal

STRENGTH OF METALS
Metals are made of many tiny crystals jumbled together. These crystals usually contain impurities and faults in the pattern of their atoms. Often, impurities are deliberately added to metals to form alloys (p. 14).

TRIAL OF STRENGTH
Test pieces made to a standard shape can be used to find out how strong different metals are.

The force of the machine causes the piece to break

SAMURAI SWORD
The aristocratic Japanese warriors known as *samurai* demanded the finest weapons. Hard, brittle steels, containing a lot of carbon, were welded by hammering on to a core of soft, low-carbon iron to produce a weapon that would stay sharp but not shatter in combat.

Slabs of impure iron

Iron is hammered to remove impurities

WROUGHT IRON
Iron straight from the blast furnace – known as cast iron – contains a lot of carbon and other impurities, which make it brittle. Before large-scale processes were developed to form strong steel by reducing the amount of carbon, cast iron was puddled to produce wrought iron. The puddling process involved adding materials such as iron oxide to molten iron, stirring it with a long paddle, then hammering it to squeeze out impurities. Wrought iron is not brittle, and it is strong in tension (pp. 20-21). The blacksmith can improve it still further by hammering it so that the grain runs in the right direction to resist the stresses it will encounter in service.

Polarized light gives false-color image

A CLOSE LOOK AT CAST IRON
Cast iron is durable, but the high carbon content makes it brittle. The etched and polished metal surface is here magnified 60 times.

Gauge to show the pressure applied

Ball is forced into the surface of the ordinary steel

BRINELL TESTER
Metals are hard as well as strong, but some are much harder than others. Hardness can be defined as the resistance of a metal to attempts to deform it. Lead, for instance, is so soft that it can be marked with the pressure of a fingernail, while some special steels are so hard they can slice through ordinary steel like butter. This machine, based on one invented in 1900 by the Swedish metallurgist Johann August Brinell (1849-1925), measures hardness precisely.

A gauge measures the width of the dent made by the testing machine

Screw to position sample

MEASURING THE INDENTATION
The width of a dent made by the testing machine is measured with a gauge and converted to a Brinell hardness number. The number for ordinary steel is 130, for example, while the aluminum used to make a frying pan has a hardness of 27. More recently, hardness has been measured using other standards such as the American Rockwell test, but the basic principle remains the same.

The end of the hammer carries a die that will fashion the top of the metal piece

The metal lies in a hollow die that will shape its underside

DROP HAMMER
Drop forging is a good way of shaping metal parts, such as car engine crankshafts, that will be highly stressed when they are in use. This huge drop hammer is like a giant mechanical blacksmith. After a few blows, the metal is roughly the right shape and can be moved to a more precisely formed part of the die for further forging. Finally, the metal, now cooler, is struck between a pair of dies that squeeze it to almost exactly the required shape.

Waste gas used as fuel

Iron ore, coke, and limestone are loaded into the furnace

Coke burns to carbon monoxide, which releases the iron from the ore

Air is blown in

Slag, or impurities, floats to the top of the iron

SMELTING
Ores consist of nonmetallic elements like oxygen or sulfur combined with the wanted metal. One way of getting rid of unwanted elements is to heat the ore with something that will combine with the elements even more strongly. Iron, for instance, is separated from the oxygen in its ore by heating it with carbon monoxide derived from coke (a form of carbon made from coal). Limestone is added to keep impurities liquid so that the iron can separate from them.

White-hot iron is tapped off, ready for further purification

Using metals

OVER 30 METALS ARE IN DAILY USE. Some are inexpensive and used widely; others are expensive, but still in demand for their special properties. Silver, for example, as well as for making jewelry, is the key ingredient in photographic film. Titanium is used in aircraft because it is light and strong, but it is also used to make white paint (pp. 50-51). Aluminum, rarely seen 100 years ago, is now the essential wrapping of most canned drinks. Many metals perform better when they are mixed with other materials to form alloys, with improved properties like higher strength or easier casting (p. 16). A most important alloy is steel, a form of iron containing a small proportion of carbon and usually some added metals. Chromium, for instance, prevents steel from rusting, while manganese gives hardness. A higher proportion of carbon gives cast iron (pp. 12-13).

Roman bronze bust

Tin

Copper

Magnified slice of bronze

THE EARLIEST ALLOY
Bronze was probably the earliest alloy in regular use, since its ingredients, copper and tin, often occur together naturally. Its fine color and resistance to corrosion makes it popular for sculpture.

VICTORIA CROSS
One of the highest decorations a British soldier can receive, the Victoria Cross, is cast from gunmetal, a type of bronze once used for making cannons. The medal was instituted by Queen Victoria in 1856. Rarely awarded, it is hung from a crimson ribbon. It was originally struck from cannons captured by the British from Russia at the battle of Sevastopol (1854-1855).

The aluminum can

The aluminum can is a remarkably clever piece of technology. It is made of a relatively expensive metal, but this is used effectively, so that a little metal wraps up a lot of drink – a modern can contains 30 percent less metal than one made 20 years ago. Consumers prefer aluminum cans for their lightness, while the highly reflective surface provides many opportunities for the packaging designer. Recycling cans is now well organized in many countries (p. 62).

THE RING-PULL TAB
This strip of ring-pull tabs in the making shows a typical sequence for stamping out small metal parts. If metals are forced too far and too fast, they tend to crack, so the blank metal strip passes under a series of presses, each of which alters it only slightly. In this way a complex shape can be formed reliably and accurately at high speeds. After the finished tabs are parted from the strip, the leftover material is recycled.

Each stamping alters the shape slightly

The finished ring-pull tab

Metal for recycling

Center bump on lid is pushed through tab and flattened

LIFT RING

PUSH BACK

Metal at the base is thicker to resist the pressure of a carbonated

The top is added after filling (below right)

Can body

Thin walls to save metal

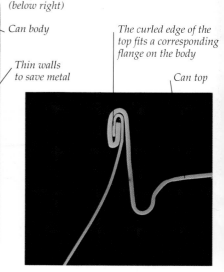

The curled edge of the top fits a corresponding flange on the body

Can top

MAKING THE CAN LID
The lid is made in a series of stamping operations. These form a bump in the center, which fits into the smaller hole in the tab and is then flattened out, forming a rivet which secures it. Before the tab is attached, a score line is cut in the lid. When the tab is pulled, the metal cracks along this line to open the can.

MAKING THE CAN BODY
A thick metal disk is forced through a hole to bend it into a cup shape. The metal is squeezed up from the base to form thin, strong walls. At the bottom, the metal stays thicker to resist the pressure of the fizzy drink.

ADDING THE TOP
Immediately it has been filled, the body receives a top and goes into a machine that rolls the two pieces of metal tightly around each other. A flexible sealant, added when the top was made, ensures no fizz escapes.

Dislocation | Atom can move into space | Atom moves slightly to relieve stress

A DISLOCATION
Metal crystals are not perfect. When they form from molten metal, a lot of atoms get caught in the wrong place as the metal sets hard. The resulting awkward gap is called a dislocation.

USEFUL MOVEMENT
Dislocations allow metals to move internally, stretching instead of cracking when they are stressed. As the atoms move, the dislocation travels across the crystal.

REPEATED STRESS
If the metal is stressed repeatedly, large numbers of shifting dislocations get in each other's way. The metal then becomes brittle, an effect known as "work hardening."

STAINLESS STEEL CUTLERY
Stainless steel was invented in 1913 by British metallurgist Harry Brearley (1871-1948). He made a steel containing 13 percent chromium. The new alloy proved to be highly resistant to corrosion: chromium reacts with oxygen in the air to form a tough, protective film which renews itself if the metal is scratched.

Stainless steel cutlery

THE BEST OF BOTH
The way metals interact with each other in alloys can be hard to predict, but sometimes a pair of different metals will blend together to give the best properties of both. This titanium-aluminum alloy, magnified about 50 times, is nearly as strong as titanium and nearly as light as aluminum. But as with most alloys, its melting point is lower than that of either metal, so for high temperatures titanium is used on its own.

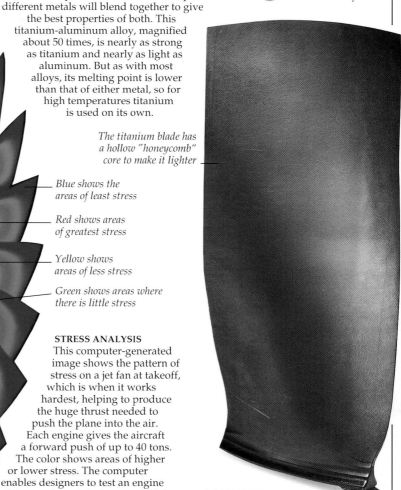

The titanium blade has a hollow "honeycomb" core to make it lighter

Blue shows the areas of least stress

Red shows areas of greatest stress

Yellow shows areas of less stress

Green shows areas where there is little stress

STRESS ANALYSIS
This computer-generated image shows the pattern of stress on a jet fan at takeoff, which is when it works hardest, helping to produce the huge thrust needed to push the plane into the air. Each engine gives the aircraft a forward push of up to 40 tons. The color shows areas of higher or lower stress. The computer enables designers to test an engine and its components before any metal is cut. Modern metals make it possible to build a lightweight structure that will withstand not only the planned stresses shown here, but also the accidental effects of a bird getting sucked into the engine. Computer design of this apparently simple component to achieve maximum efficiency has helped to reduce the cost of air travel.

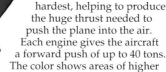

A FAN BLADE
This fan blade is from a jumbo jet engine. On takeoff, the stress on the metal is immense, as computer simulation shows (left), so to prevent the fan from flying apart, the blades must be both light and very strong. Titanium, though expensive, is the only suitable metal.

Shaping metals

METALS CAN BE SHAPED IN MORE WAYS than most other materials. They can be forced into shape while they are cold, hot, or when they are a glowing, runny liquid. Processes for shaping liquid metal – casting – have been used since metals were first discovered. The simplest, and least accurate, method is sand casting. The more expensive diecasting process forces liquid metal into a closed metal mold, or die, to make more precise components, such as those used in computers. Hollow castings can be made using an ancient technique called lost wax, or its modern equivalent, investment casting. Metal can be squeezed between rollers and also pulled through small holes to turn it into wire.

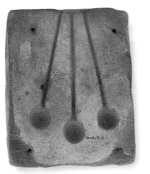

BRONZE-AGE PIN MOLD
The primitive furnaces of around 1000 BC, when this stone mold was made, were just hot enough to melt bronze (p. 14). This mold cast three decorative pins with spherical heads.

Pin

A bell foundry in Bavaria

CASTING A BELL
Church bells are made of a special bronze by lost wax casting. This allows them to be made in one piece so that there are no cracks to spoil the sound. Each bell is modeled in wax over a brick and clay core. The wax is covered with more clay, then melted out. The resulting bell-shaped cavity is filled with molten metal. After cooling and trimming, the bell is tested.

The wax patterns are dipped to coat them in clay

SAND CASTING
A place where castings are made is called a foundry. Sand casting, like sand castles, makes use of the way damp sand sticks together and forms shapes. Because sand melts at a much higher temperature than any metal, it is unaffected when molten iron or other alloys are poured in. Once the metal has solidified, the fragile sand mold is easily brushed away, leaving its shape impressed on the much more durable material.

Ladle

Molten iron is poured into the mold

Mold

INVESTMENT CASTING
Investment casting is a modern development of the ancient lost wax technique. The required shape is first cast in wax, using a metal mold, and finished by hand to remove defects. It is then sprayed or dipped to coat it with fine clay like that used to make pottery (p. 8). Once the clay is dry, it can be heated to melt away the wax, leaving a highly accurate mold that can be filled with molten metal – often a precious metal or exotic alloy.

Moist sand

Iron box

Wooden pattern

1 SHAPING THE SAND
A wooden pattern cut to the shape of one half of the casting is positioned in an iron box and surrounded by tightly packed moist sand. The pattern is then removed, leaving a precise impression of its shape like a footprint on a beach. The sand mold will be destroyed in making the casting, but the wooden pattern is not, so thousands of identical molds and castings can be made. Channels for the molten iron are also cut in the mold.

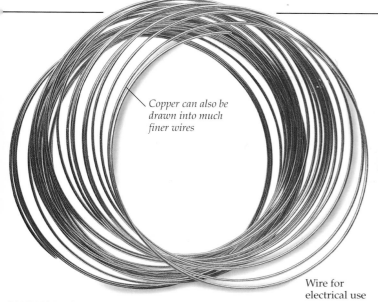

Copper can also be drawn into much finer wires

Wire for electrical use

CONDUCTING POWER
Copper wires are used everywhere to bring us light, power, and information. In metals, the electrically charged particles called electrons, which form part of every atom, are able to drift freely through the material. This makes metals like copper good conductors of electricity, so that little energy is lost when power or messages are guided through cables. Wire is made by drawing – pulling a metal strip or rod through a series of holes in hard metal, each a little smaller than the last, until it is squeezed down to size.

HOT ROLLING
When steel is heated until it glows bright red, it becomes soft enough to form into elaborate shapes. The village blacksmith uses this property when making horseshoes and ironwork of all kinds. On a larger scale, rolling mills like this can squeeze a massive strip of steel into the shape of rolled steel joists, or RSJs, used in building wherever loads must be supported over a wide gap (p. 53). The steel is passed through several sets of rollers, one after the other, each pushing the steel closer to the required shape. The final set of rollers, which work on the metal when it is relatively cool, can form it to an accurate finished size and even add the maker's name. Railroad rails are made in exactly the same way.

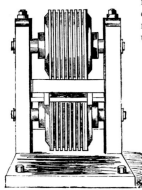

Computer connector housing

Sprue is cut off before use

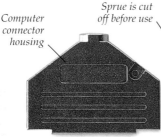

WIREMAKING ROLLERS
This 19th-century machine was used to cut sheet iron into narrow strips before it was drawn through a series of dies into the sort of wire used for such jobs as sending telegraph messages or fencing cattle.

DIECASTING COMPONENTS
Metals can be molded as precisely as plastics (p. 27) by pressure diecasting. The steel mold is made in two or more pieces. These are held together under great pressure while a precise quantity of molten metal is pumped in. When the metal has cooled, the mold opens to release a highly detailed casting which can be used right away, with very little further work, for critical parts such as these computer connectors.

Channel for molten iron

2 READY FOR THE METAL
After the wooden patterns have been removed, the two halves of the mold are clamped together. Molten iron is poured into an opening called the runner. The metal pushes out the air in the mold, which escapes through another channel called the riser. Extra metal is poured in to allow for the way metals shrink as they cool. In modern foundries, these operations are carried out by automatic machines.

3 THE FINISHED PRODUCT
This particular mold is designed to make a pair of identical castings which are used as ornaments. The little iron owls have been painted with black gloss paint to protect the iron from rusting.

COLD-ROLLED STEEL
Many modern products are made from easily shaped sheet metal (p. 14). Sheet steel or aluminum starts life as a strip around 0.2 in (5 mm) thick and 39 in (1 m) wide. The cold metal is passed through a series of rollers, each weighing several tons, which squeeze the metal down to a final thickness as small as 0.006 in (0.15 mm). Cold rolling is more accurate and gives a better finish than hot rolling. As the moving strip gets thinner, it gets longer and travels faster, reaching speeds of up to 55 mph (90 km/h).

Joining things together

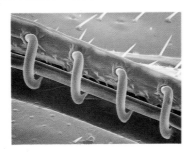

THE PRODUCTS OF TECHNOLOGY are usually made by joining together separate pieces of material. This is necessary either because different parts of the product need different properties, or because the finished shape is too big (a bridge) or complicated (a watch) to be made in any other way. There are five main methods of joining parts together. They can be perforated and something like a rivet, a bolt, or sewing thread passed through the holes. They can be coated with a material that is attracted to both surfaces, such as solder or adhesive. They can be made to flow together, as happens in welding. They can grip each other by friction, like a nail in wood. Or they can simply be shaped to lock together, like the parts of a plastic toy.

FASTENERS IN NATURE
Fasteners are needed even in nature. A bee's wing is actually two wings fastened together. Tiny hooks on the front wing lock over a bar on the back wing to form a single flying surface. On landing, the fastening is disengaged with a quick flick, allowing the bee to fold its wings.

19th-century cut nails for building work

CRUDE NAILS
Nails work best in wood, where they can force themselves between the fibers, relying on friction to keep them in place. These early cut nails were simply punched out of steel sheet.

Panel pin

Carpet tack

Round wire nail for simple carpentry

Floor brad for floorboards

Molly bolt for fixtures in hollow walls

Countersink wood screw gives neat finish

Roofing nail for holding roof felt

Staple

Countersink rivet

Roundhead rivet

Nut

Washer

Crinkle washer

Wall anchor holds screws in walls

Zinc-plated machine screw

JOINING DEVICES
Most joining devices are friction fasteners, screws, or rivets. Friction fasteners are mostly variations on the nail, but the wall anchor and molly bolt also grip by friction when their screws are tightened up. Screws and nuts also need friction to prevent them from turning and working loose, so if they are to be used where they will undergo vibration, friction has to be increased with crinkle washers or plastic inserts. Rivets are the least convenient, but the most reliable, fasteners because they pass through both the parts to be joined and then change their shape to hold the parts together permanently.

Chromium-plated wood screw

Black painted wood screw

Brass wood screw

Nail plate for joining two pieces of wood

Angle plate

Corrugated fasteners for joining corners

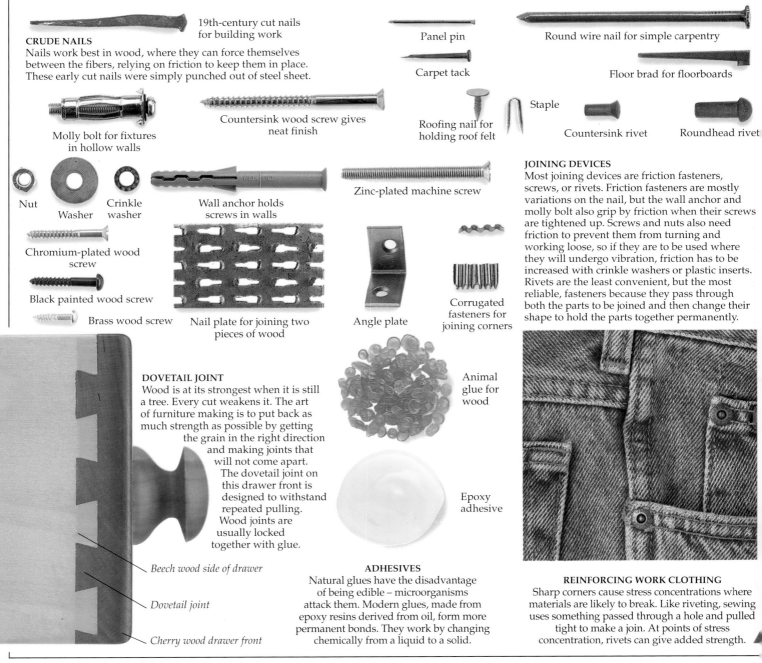

DOVETAIL JOINT
Wood is at its strongest when it is still a tree. Every cut weakens it. The art of furniture making is to put back as much strength as possible by getting the grain in the right direction and making joints that will not come apart. The dovetail joint on this drawer front is designed to withstand repeated pulling. Wood joints are usually locked together with glue.

Beech wood side of drawer

Dovetail joint

Cherry wood drawer front

Animal glue for wood

Epoxy adhesive

ADHESIVES
Natural glues have the disadvantage of being edible – microorganisms attack them. Modern glues, made from epoxy resins derived from oil, form more permanent bonds. They work by changing chemically from a liquid to a solid.

REINFORCING WORK CLOTHING
Sharp corners cause stress concentrations where materials are likely to break. Like riveting, sewing uses something passed through a hole and pulled tight to make a join. At points of stress concentration, rivets can give added strength.

RIVETING METAL

A rivet is a piece of metal like a screw with a head but no thread. It is placed in a hole drilled through two parts to be joined, and then its plain end is hammered flat from the other side to lock the parts together. This is what holds the skin of an aircraft to its frame (p. 7). Pop rivets are used where the other side is hard to reach.

1 PREPARING TO JOIN THE PARTS

The pop rivet has a hole through the middle and a steel pin running through the hole. The rivet is inserted into the head of a tool which has a handle made from a long set of levers. The rivet is then placed in a hole drilled through the two parts to be joined. The lever handle will convert a long, easy push into a shorter but much more forceful pull on the steel pin.

The steel pin runs through the hole in the rivet

SAFETY CLOTHING

Welding is often done with an acetylene gas flame. The intense heat and dazzling glare of the sparks meant that early welders were dressed from head to toe in flameproof clothing. Today, workers using electric arc welding still need a protective visor.

TIG welding join

BIKE JOINS

Tungsten inert gas (TIG) welding is the method used to join the metal parts on many modern bicycles.

The rivet is placed in the drilled holes

Pushing down on the linkage exerts a forceful pull on the pin

2 INSERTING THE RIVET

When the tool is pushed down, the head of the pin is pulled against the far end of the rivet. This squashes the end of the rivet flat and clamps together the two parts to be joined. When the rivet cannot be squeezed any further, the intense pull on the pin makes its head snap off with a "pop."

The head of the pin squashes the rivet flat

The linkage is pushed to its limit

3 THE FINISHED JOIN

The pop rivet looks neat from the outside, in spite of the hole at its center. A minor problem is that the part of the pin that snaps off is left inside.

The outside of the pop rivet

WELDING

A cut finger repairs itself by growing new skin, forming a perfect join made of the same material as the parts being joined. Welding works in much the same way. Two pieces of metal are melted with a flame or electric current and fused together along their edges, with extra metal being added for strength. Some metals, however, combine with oxygen in the air to form a tough surface film that prevents the pieces from joining. In TIG and MIG (metal inert gas) welding, this is overcome by shielding the metal with a blast of gas containing no oxygen.

Electric arc melts metal

Mask protects welder's face

Electricity and gas supply

Tension and compression

MATERIALS ARE OF NO USE UNLESS THEY CAN withstand forces. Force flows through structures like an electric current. When a structure is loaded with a weight, a force goes right through it until it reaches the Earth. The Earth then pushes upward with the same force, so the weight does not move. Without the strength to withstand pushes and pulls, even non-mechanical things like radios would stop working, because their connections would soon be torn apart. Stress – pushing or pulling – causes strain in a material. The atoms in the material move out of their normal positions, creating a force that tries to balance the pull or push. If too much force is needed, the atoms have to move so far that the material breaks. To avoid this, structures can simply be made much stronger, but this is wasteful. Engineers need to know how strong materials are, and how to work out what pushes and pulls they will encounter.

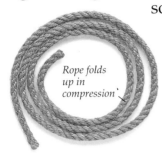

Rope folds up in compression

PUSHING ROPE
Rope can be pulled, creating tension, but it is useless where a push is needed because it cannot push back.

Rope can resist a pull

PULLING ROPE
Rope, chain, or wire can be used in tension – exerting a pulling force – as part of a structure. Wire ropes are used in suspension bridges (p. 22). But an engineer who expects tension at a certain point in a structure, and uses a rope to sustain it, had better be right. If the force turns out to be a push (compression), the rope will not be able to provide any opposing force, and the structure may collapse.

Bricks cannot resist a pull

PULLING BRICKS
Just as rope cannot resist a push, a stack of bricks cannot resist a pull – the bricks simply separate. Bricks themselves are made of small particles which are held together by quite small forces and easily pulled apart, so bricks and similar materials like concrete are weak in tension.

Bricks can resist a push

PUSHING BRICKS
Push bricks together, and they will push back with equal force: they are strong in compression. This is how walls work. The weight of the bricks, plus load like floors and the roof, forces them together to form a strong structure. The cement between the bricks merely spreads the load evenly over their surfaces.

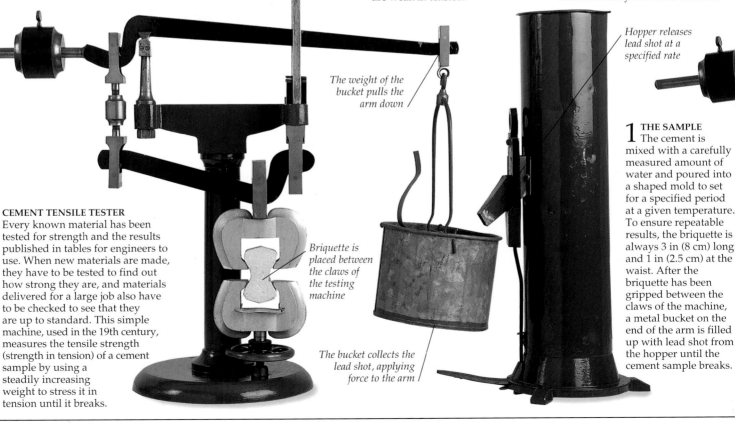

CEMENT TENSILE TESTER
Every known material has been tested for strength and the results published in tables for engineers to use. When new materials are made, they have to be tested to find out how strong they are, and materials delivered for a large job also have to be checked to see that they are up to standard. This simple machine, used in the 19th century, measures the tensile strength (strength in tension) of a cement sample by using a steadily increasing weight to stress it in tension until it breaks.

The weight of the bucket pulls the arm down

Briquette is placed between the claws of the testing machine

The bucket collects the lead shot, applying force to the arm

Hopper releases lead shot at a specified rate

1 THE SAMPLE
The cement is mixed with a carefully measured amount of water and poured into a shaped mold to set for a specified period at a given temperature. To ensure repeatable results, the briquette is always 3 in (8 cm) long and 1 in (2.5 cm) at the waist. After the briquette has been gripped between the claws of the machine, a metal bucket on the end of the arm is filled up with lead shot from the hopper until the cement sample breaks.

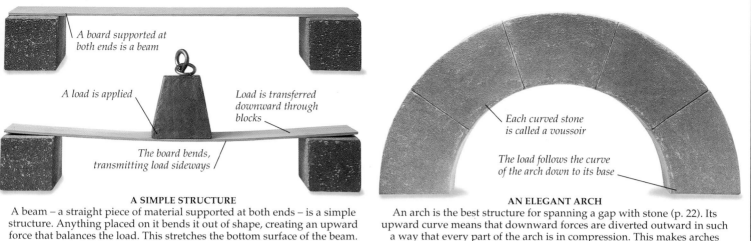

A board supported at both ends is a beam

A load is applied

Load is transferred downward through blocks

The board bends, transmitting load sideways

A SIMPLE STRUCTURE

A beam – a straight piece of material supported at both ends – is a simple structure. Anything placed on it bends it out of shape, creating an upward force that balances the load. This stretches the bottom surface of the beam. A material like stone, which breaks when stretched, is not much use for beams. All beams bend under a load, but wood bends more than steel.

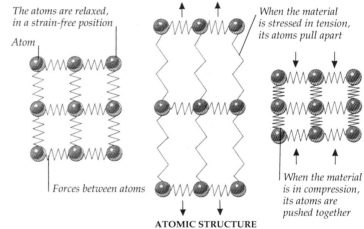

Each curved stone is called a voussoir

The load follows the curve of the arch down to its base

AN ELEGANT ARCH

An arch is the best structure for spanning a gap with stone (p. 22). Its upward curve means that downward forces are diverted outward in such a way that every part of the arch is in compression. This makes arches ideal for use with materials that have little tensile strength. Each stone, including the stone at the center, carries the same load.

BIKING MUSCLES

Traveling by bike uses less energy per mile than any other method. The bicycle gets its high efficiency from the careful application of pushes and pulls. Its frame is made from tubes, because they stand up to stresses better than solid rods of the same weight. Pushing on the pedals pulls on the chain to turn the back wheel, which pushes on the ground. However, because human push is limited, gears (pp. 32-33) are used to reduce the bicycle's speed, and therefore the push required to get up hills.

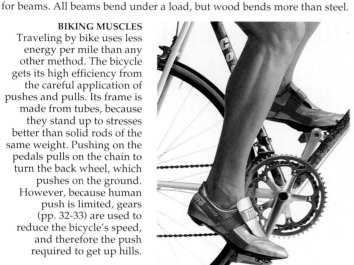

The atoms are relaxed, in a strain-free position

Atom

When the material is stressed in tension, its atoms pull apart

Forces between atoms

When the material is in compression, its atoms are pushed together

ATOMIC STRUCTURE

Solid materials always stay more or less the same shape because there are strong electrical forces attracting their atoms toward each other. One way to understand this is to imagine the atoms joined by springs. A spring can be compressed or stretched, and the farther it is pushed or pulled out of shape, the harder it resists by exerting an opposing force.

Bucket of lead shot

2 THE BRIQUETTE BREAKS

The amount of lead shot is increased until the briquette breaks, and scales are used to measure the weight of lead shot in the bucket. This weight, together with the size of the sample at its waist, can be used to calculate the tensile strength of the material. Cement is not strong in tension, which means that only a small force is needed to break it, allowing a compact laboratory machine to perform the test.

Scales weigh the lead shot needed to break the briquette

The briquette breaks under tension at its waist

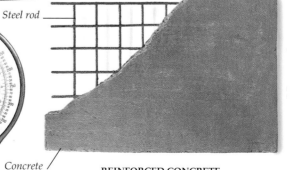

Steel rod

Concrete

REINFORCED CONCRETE

Concrete is better at resisting a push than a pull, and a thin steel rod will stand up to a big pull but buckle under a small push. Steel and concrete in partnership make a strong material that is used for most large buildings.

Building structures

THE SHEER SIZE OF BUILDINGS, DAMS, AND BRIDGES makes special demands on technology. Architects and engineers have only one chance to get things right. Detailed calculations and extensive knowledge of materials are needed to ensure that a new building will stay up, and it also has to withstand the weather and provide a comfortable environment for its occupants. Buildings should look good, too – though fashions change from age to age. Construction was simpler for builders and engineers in ancient times. Their choice of materials was limited, designs were mostly developed by modifying something done before, and taste in architecture changed only slowly. Early builders did achieve mighty works – buildings such as the great cathedrals of Europe. But these were not complex structures by the standards of a modern building, whose intricate, computer-controlled services for communication and environmental control make it as complex as a car.

PONT DU GARD
This spectacular 900-ft (275-m) structure was built by the Roman general Agrippa (*c.* 63-12 BC) about 2,000 years ago. It carried spring water over the River Gard to the town of Nîmes in France. Stone was the only material available, and the arch (p. 21) was the only structure known that allowed stone to leap a river. While the biggest arch, 95 ft (29 m) wide, is needed to clear the water, the others just help to reduce the number of stones, making the structure lighter.

HOME OF THE GLADIATORS
The Colosseum is a vast arena in Rome built in AD 70-80 from stone, brick, and concrete. The Romans were the first to use concrete on such a large scale. Arches are inserted wherever possible in the 620-ft (190-m) long building to reduce its weight.

Seating for 50,000 spectators

Four arched tiers were originally marble-faced

Ground-level chambers housed the wild animals

Concrete splay chamber — *Cable*

Steel rods embedded in concrete — *Rock*

ANCHORING A SUSPENSION BRIDGE
The cables of a suspension bridge transmit force lengthwise from the supporting towers, enabling the towers to hold up a long roadway. To avoid lengthwise forces on the towers themselves, the cables ride freely over their tops and are anchored in rock on either side of the valley being bridged. It needs elaborate anchorages like this, spreading the load over a large area of rock, to prevent the cables from breaking free.

SUSPENSION BRIDGE
Because steel is strong in tension, a roadway can be hung from steel cables held aloft by two towers. The result is a suspension bridge – a sort of upside-down arch. Impressive distances of over 1.2 miles (2 km) can be spanned this way. Thousands of years ago, primitive bridges used vines in a similar fashion to cross streams. This 1900 military suspension bridge (a model is shown here) has a span of only 200 ft (60 m) because its lightweight wooden towers could not withstand the weight of a longer bridge.

Cable anchorage

Steel ropes hold the roadway up

Wooden tower

Lightweight design could be quickly constructed, making it useful for the military

CHANNEL TUNNEL

The British half of the 31-mile (50-km) tunnel that links Britain and France was cut by this enormous machine, an engineering triumph in its own right. The entire 820-ft (250-m) monster propelled itself 250 ft (75 m) a day through the growing tunnel to meet its French counterpart 330 ft (100 m) below the surface of the English Channel in June 1991. Without the laser surveying equipment (pp. 58-59) used throughout the project, such speed and accuracy would have been impossible.

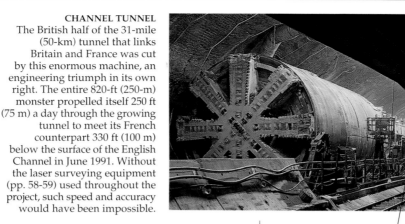

Machine carries two railroad tracks, nine computers, and ducts for air and water

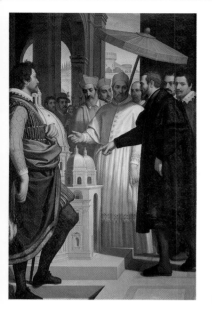

MASTER OF ALL

The Italian painter and sculptor Michelangelo (1475-1564) was one of the chief architects of the great church of St. Peter's in Rome. He is seen here showing off a model of the church to Pope Paul IV. Michelangelo's biggest contribution was the design of its superb central dome.

NEW YORK SKYSCRAPERS

In 1856 British engineer Henry Bessemer (1813-1898) invented a cheap way of making steel. This provided an answer to the problem of conserving space in North America's fast-growing cities. The height of a brick building is limited by its ability to stand up to the sideways forces imposed by wind and earth movements. But a building with a steel frame can soar to over 50 stories. The first tall steel-framed building went up in Chicago in 1885, by which time other inventions like elevators and telephones had made tall buildings practical. This view of New York shows the results.

LLOYD'S BUILDING, LONDON

British architect Richard Rogers (b. 1933) achieved instant fame in 1971 with the Pompidou Center, Paris, which saved internal space by having all its pipes and escalators on the outside. He repeated the style in 1986 with the Lloyd's Building in the City of London, which uses the inside-out idea to create a stunning interior space running the full height of the building. Permanent built-in cranes provide access for maintenance engineers. In spite of its metallic look, the building is made of concrete. How much of the gleaming steel is really needed, and how much is just there to give a hi-tech look, is something architectural critics are still arguing about.

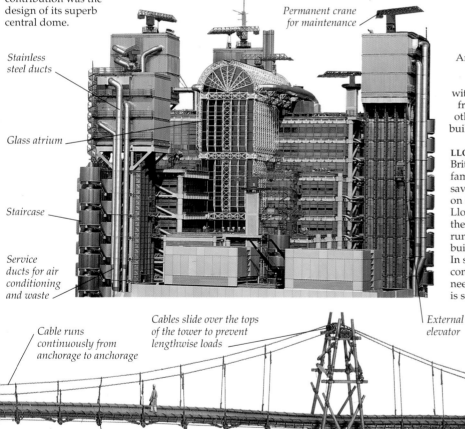

Permanent crane for maintenance

Stainless steel ducts

Glass atrium

Staircase

Service ducts for air conditioning and waste

External elevator

Cable runs continuously from anchorage to anchorage

Cables slide over the tops of the tower to prevent lengthwise loads

Each anchorage takes half the pull on the cable

Decking must be stiff to prevent dangerous vibrations

The towers take most of the weight

Wood

WOOD EVOLVED THROUGH MILLIONS OF YEARS to hold the leaves, flowers, and fruits of plants high above the ground. As soon as people had developed axes, they started to chop down trees, and wood is still one of the most widely used materials. It is used to make floors, furniture, and the paper in this book, while concrete buildings are put up by pouring cement into wooden molds. Wood is a sort of composite material (pp. 28-29) made of many long, strong, parallel fibers of cellulose. This white substance, related to sugar, is found in all plants, but in trees it is strengthened by a brown material called lignin, which gives wood its color. There are hundreds of kinds of wood, all useful for different purposes. Wood even recycles itself by rotting, producing the carbon dioxide needed for new trees. And weight for weight, this incredible material is three times as strong as steel.

MEDIEVAL AX MAN
Wood technology goes back to the Stone Age, but metal blades (pp. 12-13) were needed before woodworking could become a real craft. Even as late as 1500, a carpenter like this would rely mostly on an ax for shaping wood.

Leather used to secure the blade to the shaft

Metal blade

Cutting edge

Wooden shaft

OLD TOOL
The adze is one of the oldest woodworking tools. It was used by the ancient Egyptians to carve large wooden objects such as ships or coffins into their final shape. This ancient tool works so well that it is still in use in the Middle East today.

The blade is brought down onto the wood

NATURE'S WAY
Finland, Sweden, and Canada have vast pine forests which supply much of the world with lumber and paper. Transporting all this wood is a major expense. It can be reduced, as shown here in Canada, by the traditional method of floating the logs down a river to the sea.

Oak – used for furniture

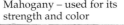
Pine – used in furniture and building

Mahogany – used for its strength and color

Ramin – used for toys and inside buildings

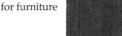
Balsa – fast growing and light

DIFFERENT WOODS
Each wood has different properties, making it better for some purposes than others. The most widely used are cheap softwoods, obtained from conifers like pine and spruce. These are grown mostly in sustainable forests where trees are replaced as they are felled. Conifers keep their leaves all year and so can grow quickly in the cold, dark forests of northern countries. Hardwoods come from slower-growing trees in warmer, brighter places. They are stronger and finer grained, but cost more. Some hardwoods, such as mahogany, are being extracted faster than they can renew themselves, threatening the survival of those species and the wildlife they support.

SMOOTHING PLANE
Wood can easily be cut with hand tools like this smoothing plane. Planing is always done with the grain, so that the fibers have only to be separated, not broken. The angle of the blade and its cutting edge are chosen to split the wood apart with the least effort, creating the familiar curly shavings. Planes are used to smooth surfaces left rough by the saw and give the wood its final dimensions.

Shavings peel off as plane moves forward

Blade is clamped in here

Adjusting screw

26279.

USING THE ADZE
The adze is halfway between an ax and a plane. It does its work by hacking into the surface of wood and then peeling away the top layer, taking advantage of the weakness of the material across the grain to produce a smooth finish.

Working with wood

Wood is strong in the direction its fibers run in, or "with the grain," but because the fibers are stuck together quite weakly it is easy to break wood "across the grain." Also, unlike metals or plastic, wood is much stronger in tension than compression (pp. 20-21), and is sensitive to moisture – swelling, or even rotting, in a damp atmosphere. The design of wooden objects has to allow for this. Most older furniture and many musical instruments are made from wood. A violin, for example, is a remarkable piece of cutting, shaping, and joining that makes mute lumber sing.

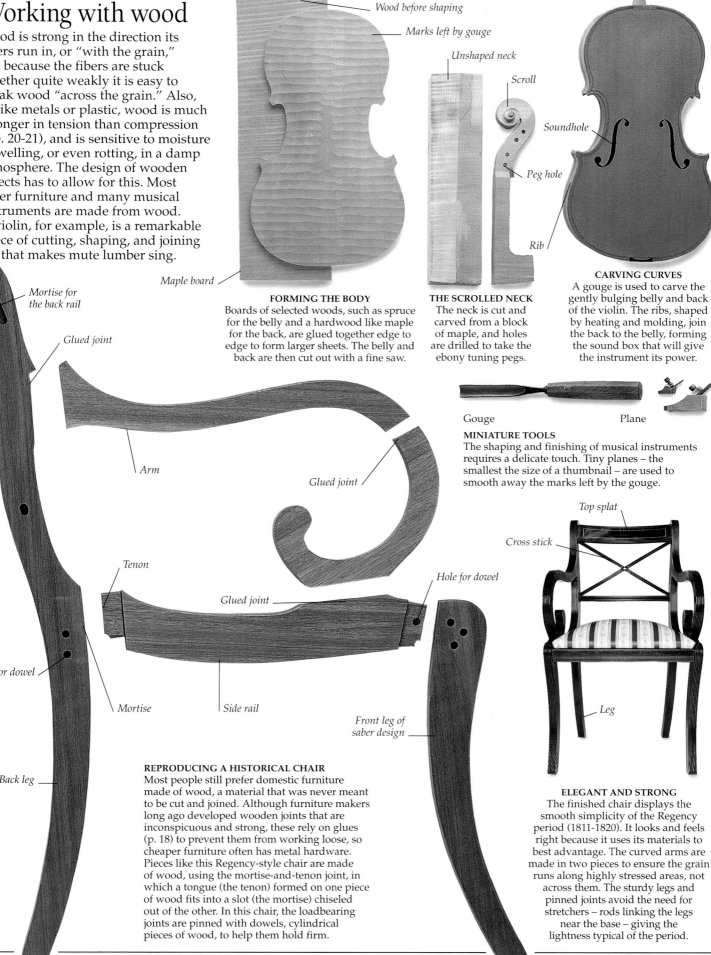

Wood before shaping

Marks left by gouge

Unshaped neck

Scroll

Soundhole

Peg hole

Rib

Maple board

FORMING THE BODY
Boards of selected woods, such as spruce for the belly and a hardwood like maple for the back, are glued together edge to edge to form larger sheets. The belly and back are then cut out with a fine saw.

THE SCROLLED NECK
The neck is cut and carved from a block of maple, and holes are drilled to take the ebony tuning pegs.

CARVING CURVES
A gouge is used to carve the gently bulging belly and back of the violin. The ribs, shaped by heating and molding, join the back to the belly, forming the sound box that will give the instrument its power.

Gouge

Plane

MINIATURE TOOLS
The shaping and finishing of musical instruments requires a delicate touch. Tiny planes – the smallest the size of a thumbnail – are used to smooth away the marks left by the gouge.

Mortise for the back rail

Glued joint

Arm

Glued joint

Top splat

Cross stick

Tenon

Hole for dowel

Glued joint

Hole for dowel

Mortise

Side rail

Front leg of saber design

Leg

Back leg

REPRODUCING A HISTORICAL CHAIR
Most people still prefer domestic furniture made of wood, a material that was never meant to be cut and joined. Although furniture makers long ago developed wooden joints that are inconspicuous and strong, these rely on glues (p. 18) to prevent them from working loose, so cheaper furniture often has metal hardware. Pieces like this Regency-style chair are made of wood, using the mortise-and-tenon joint, in which a tongue (the tenon) formed on one piece of wood fits into a slot (the mortise) chiseled out of the other. In this chair, the loadbearing joints are pinned with dowels, cylindrical pieces of wood, to help them hold firm.

ELEGANT AND STRONG
The finished chair displays the smooth simplicity of the Regency period (1811-1820). It looks and feels right because it uses its materials to best advantage. The curved arms are made in two pieces to ensure the grain runs along highly stressed areas, not across them. The sturdy legs and pinned joints avoid the need for stretchers – rods linking the legs near the base – giving the lightness typical of the period.

Plastics

SPIDER IN AMBER
Amber is a natural plastic, the fossilized resin of a pine tree. When first formed, this chunk of amber was a sticky liquid. The spider it trapped is now preserved forever.

NATURAL PLASTICS LIKE PINE RESIN have existed for millions of years, but in the 1850s chemists started trying to make artificial plastics. Most plastics are easily shaped by heat. Some are more transparent than glass, some stronger than steel, some stiff, some soft. They can be spun into fibers, squirted or squeezed into tubes or sheets, or fizzed into foams. The first synthetic plastic was invented by the British chemist Alexander Parkes (1813-1890) in about 1855. This material was eventually improved upon in the US to give celluloid, the flexible, transparent (but explosively flammable) material that made movies possible. These early products were the beginning of a revolution in materials that now touches every aspect of life.

The granules are colored with pigments

THE RAW MATERIAL
These molding granules are fed into a machine that can melt them to a syrupy liquid and force them into the shape of a metal mold in just a few seconds (p. 38). Materials of this kind are called thermoplastic, because they soften when heated ("thermo" refers to heat and "plastic" means "easy to mold").

LISTENING TO MUSIC
This mechanical record player, or gramophone, from the 1920s, is a reminder of how much plastics have improved things. Its body is made of flat pieces of wood, giving it a boxy shape, and its moving parts and horn are made of metal, so it is very heavy. The record it plays is made of a primitive plastic: a natural resin called shellac, strengthened with powdered slate and carbon. This molds well, but breaks easily, while its coarse texture gives a scratchy sound and limits playing time to a few minutes.

Sound reflector

Metal needle lasts for one play

Shellac record

Brake

Metal horn

Box of spare needles

Wooden box covered with imitation leather

Handle used to wind up the motor

LONG-PLAYING RECORD
Sound recording was invented in 1877, and at first used cylindrical records made of wax. Flat records, invented by German engineer Emile Berliner (1851-1929) in 1887, could be molded with early plastics. But PVC, or vinyl, available from the 1940s, was smoother, allowing finer grooves and a slower playing speed.

COMPACT DISC
Compact discs, which first appeared in 1982, would not exist without modern plastics. The original recording is made on plastic tape, using electronics (p. 58) that depends on plastics. The disc is made of a tough, transparent plastic called polycarbonate. It is injection molded (p. 38) using a laser-cut tool that impresses it with billions of tiny pits, each one hundreds of times narrower than a period, which carry the music in coded form.

Using plastics

Plastics are called polymers, from the Greek *poly* (many) and *mer* (part), because their long molecules are made of the same simple pattern of atoms repeated over and over again. They can now be tailored to almost any task. Most plastics soften with heat, but some get harder. These are thermosetting plastics. The first was Bakelite, invented in 1907 by Belgian chemist Leo Baekeland (1863-1944).

THE PLASTIC BAG
This bag starts as a continuous roll of material, made by blowing air into the molten plastic to form a tube. After printing, this is cut into short lengths and shaped into bags.

Metal handle

Bakelite can be molded to complex shapes

Bakelite is always dark in color

1920s vacuum jug

BAKELITE VACUUM FLASK
Bakelite was the first thermosetting plastic. Its dark color limited its use. Thermosetting plastics are molded by squeezing a resin dough in a heated press.

Molecules link together

THERMOSETTING PLASTICS
Thermosetting plastics harden because heat gives their molecules the energy they need to link together into a rigid mesh. Some other materials, like epoxy resin used for gluing metals (p. 18), set in a similar way by means of a chemical reaction that can occur at room temperature.

Acrylic plastic eye

CHILDREN'S TOY
This cuddly toy is made with the same plastics used for aircraft windows and beverage bottles. Its soft acrylic fur is made by squirting the plastic through tiny holes to form fibers, which are then woven into a backing material. In sheet form, however, acrylics are stiff and transparent, just right for windows. This bear is stuffed with fiber made of polyester, a plastic also used for bottles, fabric, and rope.

The bear is stuffed with polyester fiber

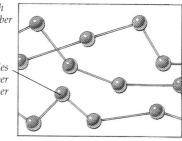

Molecules slide over each other

THERMOPLASTIC POLYMER
In a thermoplastic, the molecules are normally tangled together to form a solid. But when the material is heated, they gain enough energy to slide over each other, forming a sticky liquid.

The fur is made from an acrylic fabric

Nylon velvet paw

Cellulose triacetate film

MAKING MOVIES
Celluloid appeared in 1887. It was the first tough, transparent material that could be rolled up and fed through a camera. Modern films are made of cellulose triacetate which, unlike its ancestor celluloid, will not catch fire or explode.

MOLDING PLASTIC
The most common technique for molding thermoplastics is injection molding (p. 38), in which molten plastic is forced into closed steel molds. Good mold design ensures that products will be the right size, and related parts like these can be made in one shot.

RUBBER FOR BABIES
Some plastics have long, stretchy molecules and are called elastomers. Rubber is a natural elastomer that comes from trees. In its unprocessed form, it is known as latex and used wherever a tough, flexible material is needed, as in this nipple for a baby's bottle.

The sprue is an impression of the channel through which the plastic was fed

This pair of electrical components, when separated, will fit together perfectly

PLASTIC ROAD
Expanded polystyrene (polystyrene blown up with millions of tiny gas bubbles) appeared in the 1950s. It can replace the normal rubble infill in the bed of a road. It is lighter than stone and comes in neat blocks, so it can be laid quickly and cheaply.

Composite materials

MATERIALS CAN OFTEN BE IMPROVED by putting two of them together, so that each makes up for the deficiencies of the other. In this way several excellent, inexpensive materials have been created that make better products available at lower cost. Composites are usually made from pairs of materials that have opposite properties. One is often in the form of strands or fibers, which though strong in tension are too floppy to stand up to being compressed (pp. 20-21). The other material can then be something that will simply stick the fibers together. Often this second material, or "matrix," is quite weak or brittle, but a crack that starts running through the material, threatening to break it, will get diverted sideways if it hits a fiber. This reduces the stress that is causing the crack, so the crack stops.

FLAK JACKET
This UN soldier is wearing a flak jacket that will stop a bullet, although it contains nothing stronger than thin sheets of plastic. This composite material illustrates the ability of multiple layers to divert dangerous energy.

Plastic sheets

Fabric layers

Bullet

HOW LAYERS STOP A BULLET
When a bullet strikes a stack of thin sheets weakly glued together, they separate from each other over a wide area. It takes energy to do this, energy which otherwise would have punched a hole. In composite materials, tiny fibers suspended in a matrix of a different material can produce the same effect.

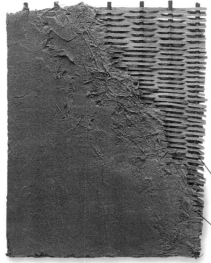

Interwoven strips of wattle

Mud (daub) smeared on to lock the strips in place

Narrow racing saddle for freedom of movement

Carbon-fiber frame is molded as a single hollow shell

Gears are not required on a pursuit track

SLOW AND GENTLE GAME
A tennis racquet needs to be light and stiff. If it bends too much when the ball hits it, energy is lost and the return stroke will be weak, while a heavy racquet slows the player down. Early tennis racquets were made of wood, a natural composite, steamed and bent to shape in several layers. The result was fairly stiff but rather heavy.

Handle is filled with plastic foam to improve balance

WATTLE AND DAUB
Ancient peoples often combined natural fibers with mud or plaster to make bricks and other parts of buildings. A simple form of this technique was wattle and daub. Each material contributed its strengths to compensate for the other's weaknesses.

Rear wheel has no spokes, cutting down wind resistance

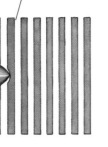

The metal is melted out after molding to leave a hollow frame

UNBEATABLE MATERIAL
Fibers of pure carbon, made by turning cellulose fibers into charcoal, are stiffer than any other material of the same weight. Mixing them with nylon, a tough plastic, makes graphite, an unbeatable material for sports equipment. Racquets like this are made by molding graphite around a metal core that is then melted out.

MAVIC

Chain

Lightweight alloy crank and pedals

GLASS-REINFORCED PLASTIC CHAIR

The flowing curves of this 1960s chair are made possible by a composite usually known as fiberglass, although fine strands of glass are only one of its components. The fibers can resist pulls, but not pushes, so they are set into a plastic matrix that supplies the missing compressive strength, as well as giving a smooth, shiny surface. The plastic is not particularly strong, but the fibers embedded in it have immense strength once they have been protected from buckling by the surrounding plastic. Any crack that does start will soon be blunted and stopped by running into a fiber.

GLASS PROTECTION

Laminated glass is a simple composite. It consists of a layer of tough plastic glued between two sheets of glass. The glass protects the plastic from cuts and scratches, while the plastic prevents the glass from shattering when struck by a missile. Most modern aircraft, however, use acrylic sheets because glass is too heavy.

Second World War fighter planes needed bulletproof glass

Foam core

Honeycomb trailing edge reduces weight

minated plastic leading edge

A BLADE FROM A HELICOPTER

This helicopter rotor blade is a complex structure containing both glass and carbon fibers. It is denser on the outside, where it is highly stressed, with foam and honeycomb structures inside to reduce the weight while providing the necessary stiffness. Using composite blades overcomes the problem of metal fatigue, in which metals are weakened and broken by the sort of continual flexing these blades experience in service.

Glossy surface of plastic containing no fibers

Crack

Resin holds fibers together and prevents them from buckling

Chopped fiber arranged randomly

Forearm rest

Hand grips

FIBER COMPOSITES

Fibers are enormously strong, but they need to be supported and stuck together if they are to form useful products. In both glass and carbon reinforced materials, plastics hold the fibers together and prevent them from buckling. If a crack forms, fibers divert it so the crack does not run through the material and break it.

Narrow tires reduce rolling resistance

GOLD-MEDAL BICYCLE

This revolutionary bicycle, made from a carbon-fiber composite, powered British cyclist Chris Boardman to gold in the 1992 Olympic 2.5-mile (4,000-m) pursuit. Normally, plastics are too floppy to make a good bike, but the new material makes this machine stiffer, lighter, and more aerodynamic. The one-piece, or monocoque, molded frame makes a much better mount for wheels, pedals, and rider than the traditional arrangement of welded metal tubes. Built for competition, the bicycle has no brakes or gears. The uncomfortable riding position reduces wind drag on the rider.

Spaces allow wind through when wheel is at an angle

Measurements

Each carob seed weighs about the same

The seed pod

HONEST SEEDS
In ancient times it was difficult to convince customers that weights had not been tampered with, so seeds of the carob tree were often used as a measure. Their weight could not be greatly changed without obvious damage.

18 carat gold

MEASURING A GOLD RING
The percentage of gold in an alloy is often expressed as the number of carats per ounce. There are 24 carats in an ounce, so 24-carat gold is the pure metal, while 18-carat gold is only $^{18}\!/_{24}$ or 75 percent gold.

A CAR CONTAINS THOUSANDS OF PARTS made in many different countries. Because of accurate measurement, they all get to the factory and fit together perfectly. Universal standards of size, position, weight, electrical properties, and even color (pp. 50-51) have been distributed all over the world, making expensive handcrafting of products in a single workshop unnecessary. Measurement in industry goes well beyond the capabilities of the familiar tape measure, clock, and kitchen scales. Mechanical parts accurate to 0.001 in (0.025 mm) have been common for 100 years. Optical parts deviate less than 0.00001 in (0.00025 mm) from their true curve, yet are made cheaply in the thousands. Navigation by sea and air has been transformed by global positioning satellites that hang in space to pinpoint ships and planes. For radios and satellites to work, time must be measured to within less than a second a century so that there is no buildup of errors.

Standard liter (35.2 fl oz)

Standard half liter or 500 ml (17.6 fl oz)

Standard 100 ml (3.5 fl oz)

Standard 10 ml (0.35 fl oz)

METRIC MEASURES
The metric system was introduced in France in 1795 during the French Revolution. It replaced many conflicting length and mass standards with just two, the meter and the gram. A separate unit, the liter, was defined as the volume of 1 kg (2.2 lb) of water. Standard liter measures like these were used in the 19th century to ensure accuracy in measuring jugs.

The container for the cubic inch

Accurate cubic inch (16.4 cu cm)

A CUBIC INCH
Technology depends on measurement, as well as providing it. The properties of materials have to be known precisely so that designers can make useful calculations. This accurate standard, machined from brass and nickel plated, was used in 1889 by the British Board of Trade to find the weight of a cubic inch (16 ml) of pure water. It is shown here about 1.7 times its actual size.

DISTILLER'S COPPER MEASURE
This splendid jug was made in 1910 for selling alcoholic beverages in bulk. It is one of a set covering quantities from 2 gallons (9 liters) to 1 pint (0.6 liter). The volume is correct when it is filled up to the narrowest part. Inside the spout is the seal of the City of London, certifying its accuracy.

Half yard mark

BRONZE YARD (1497)
The imperial system of measurement originated with the Romans. Parts of it survive in Britain, and a slightly different version is still used in the US. Its length standard is the yard, which is divided into 3 feet, each of 12 inches. The precision of this official yard is poor by modern standards, where lengths are defined by laser light (p. 59), but it was good enough for the technology of its day.

Inch mark

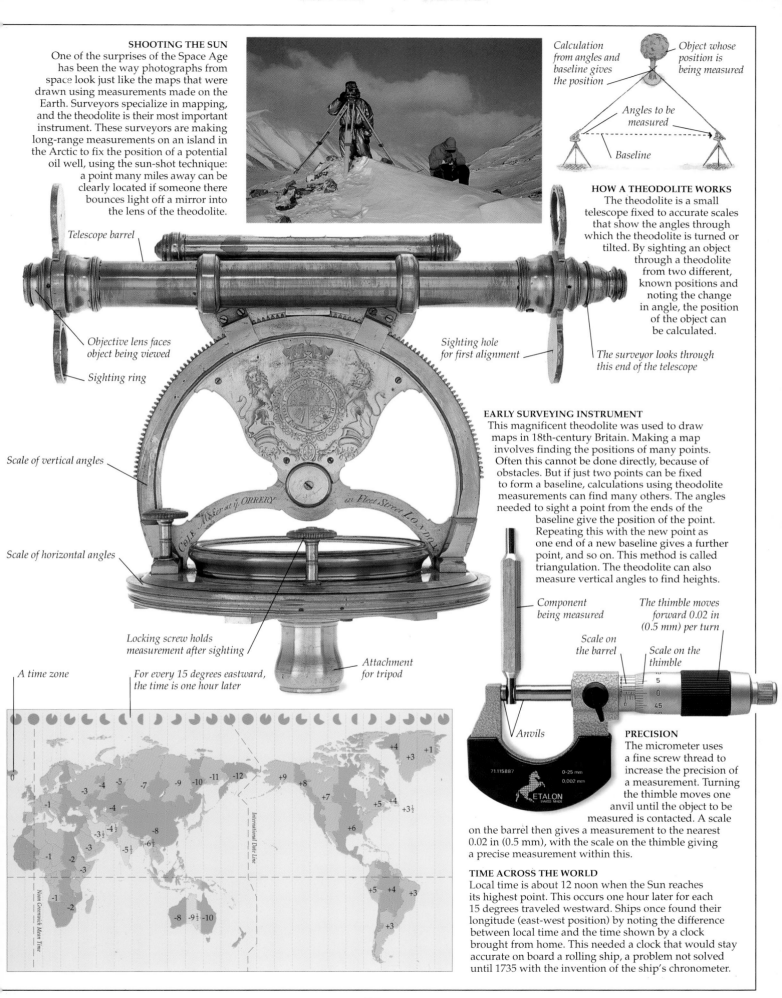

SHOOTING THE SUN
One of the surprises of the Space Age has been the way photographs from space look just like the maps that were drawn using measurements made on the Earth. Surveyors specialize in mapping, and the theodolite is their most important instrument. These surveyors are making long-range measurements on an island in the Arctic to fix the position of a potential oil well, using the sun-shot technique: a point many miles away can be clearly located if someone there bounces light off a mirror into the lens of the theodolite.

Calculation from angles and baseline gives the position

Object whose position is being measured

Angles to be measured

Baseline

HOW A THEODOLITE WORKS
The theodolite is a small telescope fixed to accurate scales that show the angles through which the theodolite is turned or tilted. By sighting an object through a theodolite from two different, known positions and noting the change in angle, the position of the object can be calculated.

Telescope barrel

Objective lens faces object being viewed

Sighting ring

Sighting hole for first alignment

The surveyor looks through this end of the telescope

Scale of vertical angles

Scale of horizontal angles

EARLY SURVEYING INSTRUMENT
This magnificent theodolite was used to draw maps in 18th-century Britain. Making a map involves finding the positions of many points. Often this cannot be done directly, because of obstacles. But if just two points can be fixed to form a baseline, calculations using theodolite measurements can find many others. The angles needed to sight a point from the ends of the baseline give the position of the point. Repeating this with the new point as one end of a new baseline gives a further point, and so on. This method is called triangulation. The theodolite can also measure vertical angles to find heights.

Component being measured

The thimble moves forward 0.02 in (0.5 mm) per turn

Scale on the barrel

Scale on the thimble

Locking screw holds measurement after sighting

Attachment for tripod

Anvils

PRECISION
The micrometer uses a fine screw thread to increase the precision of a measurement. Turning the thimble moves one anvil until the object to be measured is contacted. A scale on the barrel then gives a measurement to the nearest 0.02 in (0.5 mm), with the scale on the thimble giving a precise measurement within this.

TIME ACROSS THE WORLD
Local time is about 12 noon when the Sun reaches its highest point. This occurs one hour later for each 15 degrees traveled westward. Ships once found their longitude (east-west position) by noting the difference between local time and the time shown by a clock brought from home. This needed a clock that would stay accurate on board a rolling ship, a problem not solved until 1735 with the invention of the ship's chronometer.

A time zone

For every 15 degrees eastward, the time is one hour later

Ingenious mechanisms

IN AN AGE OF ELECTRONICS, moving parts still matter. A personal computer has several motors whirring around inside it. The printer has yet more motors, plus clever mechanisms to handle the paper and form the image on it. Electronic watches still have hands operated by ratchets – toothed wheels that are pushed around one tooth at a time. The wheel is often thought of as the first mechanism to be invented, but levers and wedges are much older. All mechanisms are built from just a few kinds of parts, which either transmit or store energy or information, allow smooth movement, or guide motion. Power can be transmitted with mechanical advantage by levers, gears, and pulleys, which are able to convert a small force into a larger one by turning a large movement into a smaller one.

STAIR PUPPET
Mechanisms are a way of forcing energy to do what we want. A staircase allows us to get rid of energy in small controlled bundles as we step down rather than fall down. This toy makes use of stairs by converting each burst of energy into an amusing motion. The puppets move in a humanlike way because human skeletons, like the puppets, are made of levers hinged together.

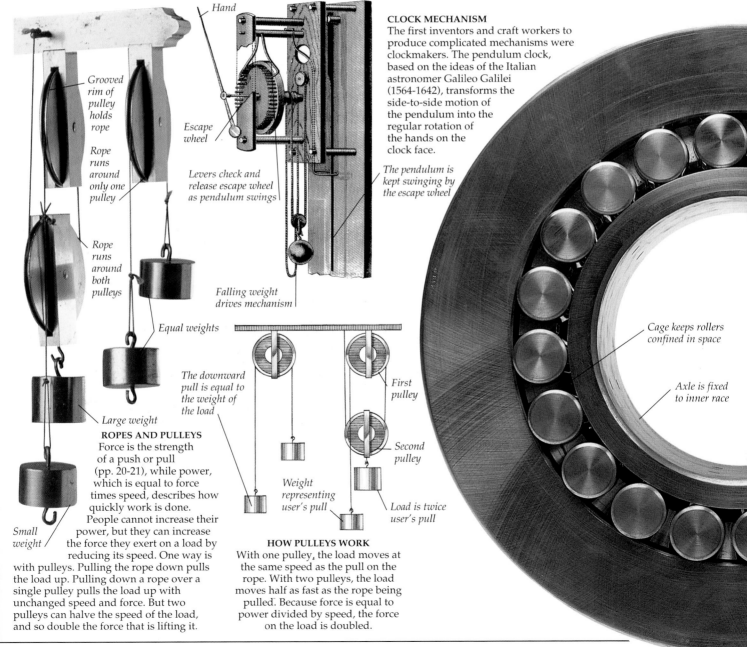

Hand

Grooved rim of pulley holds rope

Rope runs around only one pulley

Escape wheel

Levers check and release escape wheel as pendulum swings

Rope runs around both pulleys

Equal weights

Large weight

Small weight

CLOCK MECHANISM
The first inventors and craft workers to produce complicated mechanisms were clockmakers. The pendulum clock, based on the ideas of the Italian astronomer Galileo Galilei (1564-1642), transforms the side-to-side motion of the pendulum into the regular rotation of the hands on the clock face.

The pendulum is kept swinging by the escape wheel

Falling weight drives mechanism

The downward pull is equal to the weight of the load

First pulley

Second pulley

Weight representing user's pull

Load is twice user's pull

Cage keeps rollers confined in space

Axle is fixed to inner race

ROPES AND PULLEYS
Force is the strength of a push or pull (pp. 20-21), while power, which is equal to force times speed, describes how quickly work is done. People cannot increase their power, but they can increase the force they exert on a load by reducing its speed. One way is with pulleys. Pulling the rope down pulls the load up. Pulling down a rope over a single pulley pulls the load up with unchanged speed and force. But two pulleys can halve the speed of the load, and so double the force that is lifting it.

HOW PULLEYS WORK
With one pulley, the load moves at the same speed as the pull on the rope. With two pulleys, the load moves half as fast as the rope being pulled. Because force is equal to power divided by speed, the force on the load is doubled.

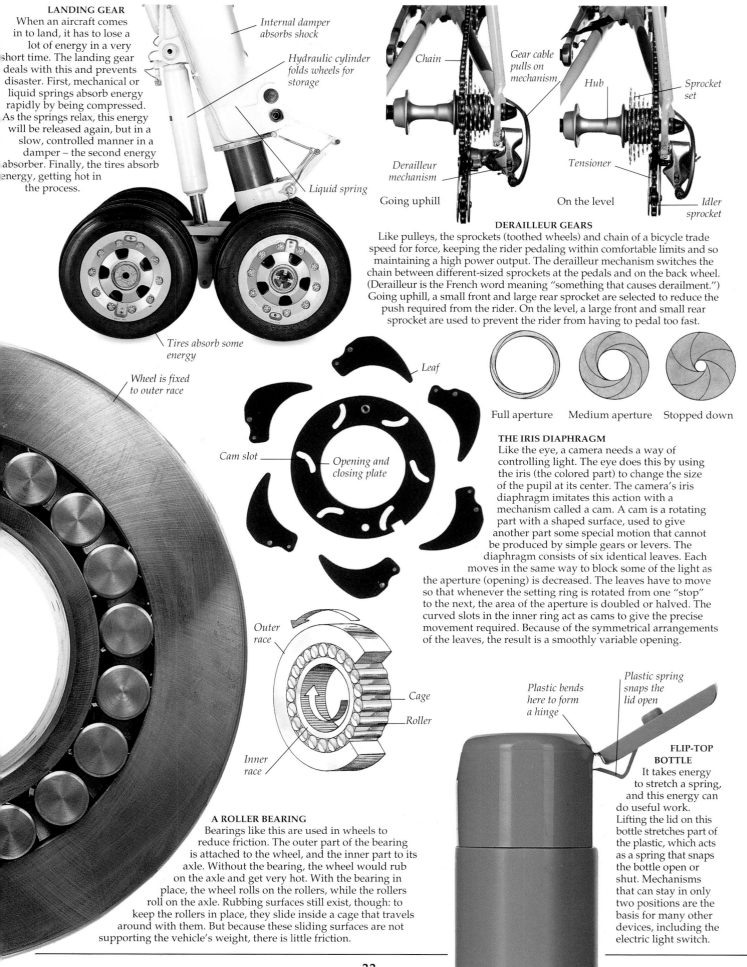

LANDING GEAR

When an aircraft comes in to land, it has to lose a lot of energy in a very short time. The landing gear deals with this and prevents disaster. First, mechanical or liquid springs absorb energy rapidly by being compressed. As the springs relax, this energy will be released again, but in a slow, controlled manner in a damper – the second energy absorber. Finally, the tires absorb energy, getting hot in the process.

Internal damper absorbs shock

Hydraulic cylinder folds wheels for storage

Liquid spring

Tires absorb some energy

Wheel is fixed to outer race

Chain

Gear cable pulls on mechanism

Hub

Sprocket set

Derailleur mechanism

Tensioner

Going uphill

On the level

Idler sprocket

DERAILLEUR GEARS

Like pulleys, the sprockets (toothed wheels) and chain of a bicycle trade speed for force, keeping the rider pedaling within comfortable limits and so maintaining a high power output. The derailleur mechanism switches the chain between different-sized sprockets at the pedals and on the back wheel. (Derailleur is the French word meaning "something that causes derailment.") Going uphill, a small front and large rear sprocket are selected to reduce the push required from the rider. On the level, a large front and small rear sprocket are used to prevent the rider from having to pedal too fast.

Leaf

Cam slot

Opening and closing plate

Full aperture   Medium aperture   Stopped down

THE IRIS DIAPHRAGM

Like the eye, a camera needs a way of controlling light. The eye does this by using the iris (the colored part) to change the size of the pupil at its center. The camera's iris diaphragm imitates this action with a mechanism called a cam. A cam is a rotating part with a shaped surface, used to give another part some special motion that cannot be produced by simple gears or levers. The diaphragm consists of six identical leaves. Each moves in the same way to block some of the light as the aperture (opening) is decreased. The leaves have to move so that whenever the setting ring is rotated from one "stop" to the next, the area of the aperture is doubled or halved. The curved slots in the inner ring act as cams to give the precise movement required. Because of the symmetrical arrangements of the leaves, the result is a smoothly variable opening.

Outer race

Cage

Roller

Inner race

A ROLLER BEARING

Bearings like this are used in wheels to reduce friction. The outer part of the bearing is attached to the wheel, and the inner part to its axle. Without the bearing, the wheel would rub on the axle and get very hot. With the bearing in place, the wheel rolls on the rollers, while the rollers roll on the axle. Rubbing surfaces still exist, though: to keep the rollers in place, they slide inside a cage that travels around with them. But because these sliding surfaces are not supporting the vehicle's weight, there is little friction.

Plastic bends here to form a hinge

Plastic spring snaps the lid open

FLIP-TOP BOTTLE

It takes energy to stretch a spring, and this energy can do useful work. Lifting the lid on this bottle stretches part of the plastic, which acts as a spring that snaps the bottle open or shut. Mechanisms that can stay in only two positions are the basis for many other devices, including the electric light switch.

The factory

THE PURPOSE OF THE FACTORY was to gather groups of workers together around powered machines that could do things previously done by hand. Factory work also allowed people to be better organized, with less time wasted in switching between different tasks. This led to Henry Ford's mass production system (p. 42), still in use today. Although early factory owners were not generous, their workers could still earn more than at home or on a farm, and factory work eventually became the way most people earned a living.

(p. 42)

ENGLISH POTTER
Josiah Wedgwood (1730-1795) was among the first to organize his workers for efficient production. He installed the first steam engine in a factory. Wedgwood also developed several uniquely beautiful and practical kinds of pottery, such as the famous Wedgwood blue Jasperware.

Molded figure applied by hand

Jasperware cup (1994)

Bell to summon workers

Gears transmit power to parts of the factory

Weaving loom

WATER POWER
It was water that got the Industrial Revolution going in the 18th century and created the factories that made the modern world. Water rushing through wheels like this provided the power to operate spinning machines and looms in textile mills, while water in canals provided a transportation system that was much better than rutted roads. Developments like these made factories inevitable. Business people who could gather workers together to make full use of the new inventions quickly put their less adventurous rivals out of business. In the 18th century, as now, it was access to energy and communications that decided success or failure.

Water flows under the mill, turning the wheel

Model of water wheel in an 18th-century cotton mill

POWER FOR THE POTTERIES
These 19th-century bottle kilns (so called because of their shape) are of a type that was still in use until the early years of the 20th century. Fuel was burned beneath a brick floor carrying the unfired pottery. Holes in the floor allowed hot gases from the fire to heat the pots and escape through the chimney. Loading, firing, and unloading took days. This way of using fuel was wasteful. Modern kilns are fired by gas or electricity.

KARL MARX (1818-1883)
The development of factories led to the rise of a capitalist class – people who took the risks in new factory enterprises. If they succeeded, they grew rich from the labor of their workers. In his book of 1867, *Das Kapital* ("Capital"), German thinker Karl Marx stated that capitalism could increase material wealth but also breed resentment, and so could not last. He inspired the communist revolutions of the 20th century.

THE VENICE ARSENALE
The principles of organized production were understood long before factories were established. On a modern production line, the work comes to the worker, who constantly repeats the same operation. But the idea can be reversed, with the work staying put and the worker moving. This was how the medieval Arsenale shipyard in Venice, Italy, was able to sustain the fantastic output of ships needed in the wars that occupied rival states for centuries before Italy became one nation. When the ships finally moved out into the canal, they were loaded with items from the windows of the Arsenale, allowing a ship to be made ready to sail in 24 hours.

Mechanization of work

Work began to be mechanized in the middle of the 18th century after thousands of years when nearly everything was done by hand. This was, perhaps, because the successes of science and mathematics in understanding nature gave people the confidence to try out new ideas. Some enterprising factory owners made a start with improved ways of making things, using machines worked by water power. The truly ancient crafts of spinning and weaving were among the first to be tackled. The new machines quickly led to mass production of cloth (pp. 38-39), so wool and cotton garments became much cheaper.

FORMING THE YARN
Spinning is the process by which the fibers of wool or cotton are twisted together to form the thread or yarn used to weave cloth. Before mechanization, this was done by hand using a spindle. One hand twirls the beginnings of the yarn, from which the weighted spindle is hung, so that fibers from a bundle held in the other hand are drawn out and twisted. This slow and erratic process became obsolete with the introduction of the spinning wheel from India around the 13th century.

THE SPINNING FRAME
The water frame, invented by the British textile pioneer Richard Arkwright (1732-1792) in 1769, took the mechanization of spinning, begun by the traditional spinning wheel, two stages further. It spun the yarn with a mechanism just like that of the spinning wheel (operating vertically instead of horizontally). It also mechanized the feeding of unspun fiber and was designed to be power driven – in this case by water. These two innovations meant that spinning could be done quickly by someone with little training.

Roller draws out thread ready for spinning

Partly spun thread

Hoop-shaped flyer rotates to spin yarn

Bobbin to hold finished yarn

The fibers are teased out with the fingers and twisted as the spindle rotates

The spindle is rotated

Pulley transmits power

Weight pulls out the yarn and keeps the spindle spinning

BELT-DRIVEN FACTORY (1900)
Power in this textile mill reached the looms through leather belts driven from shafts stretching the length of the building. The belts often broke, wasting energy and causing injuries. In the early 20th century electric generators and motors were installed in some factories, making them safer and more efficient.

MECHANIZATION FOR SPEED AND CHEAPNESS
One of the ways to speed up operations is to process articles many at a time. A tailor making a suit to fit an individual customer cuts out single pieces of cloth with scissors. This factory, making clothes to sell off the rack, cuts them out by the hundred using a laser beam. The laser (pp. 58-59), guided by a computer that holds a digital description of the required shapes, can cut through many layers of fabric without stretching them.

Heat engines

HOW A ROCKET WORKS
When a rocket pushes its burning fuel out backward, the rocket itself gets pushed forward.

HEAT AND THE MOTION OF OBJECTS are both forms of energy. A heat engine converts one into the other. This feat was first managed on a large scale by the British engineer Thomas Newcomen (1663-1729) in 1712, who produced a steam engine for pumping water. Steam turbines (machines turned by steam pushing past fan blades) now drive electric generators to provide much of the world's energy. A heat engine is judged by the percentage of heat it converts into work and the power it gives relative to its weight. Heat can be converted more directly into work by burning the fuel in contact with the moving parts of the engine, as in the internal combustion engine and the jet engine.

EARLY STEAM ENGINES
Steam engines eventually became light enough and powerful enough to heave themselves along on their own wheels, but only on specially built, smooth, level surfaces – railroads. The first rail locomotive ran in 1801, but it was the *Rocket* of 1829, built by British engineer Robert Stephenson (1803-1859), that proved railroads would really work.

INTERNAL COMBUSTION ENGINE
A steam engine works in two stages: a fire in a boiler produces steam, and then this expands in a cylinder to do the work. By the mid-19th century, people were experimenting with smaller, more efficient engines that did away with steam by putting the fire inside the cylinder itself. There were problems finding a suitable fuel, getting it into the engine, and setting fire to it. These were all solved by the German engineer Nikolaus Otto (1832-1891). He built the first gas engine in 1861 and followed this up with the four-stroke engine, the ancestor of the modern car engine, in 1876. Otto used an electric spark to ignite the mixture of fuel and air. In 1893 another German engineer, Rudolph Diesel (1858-1913), produced an engine in which the mixture is made to explode simply by being compressed. Diesel engines are heavier but more reliable and economical than gas engines.

Camshaft controls the valves

Cam

Piston ring seals the piston to prevent gases from escaping

Air intake

Valve lets fuel and air in and exhaust gases out

Alternator

Belt drives alternator to supply electricity to spark plugs

Crankshaft turns the piston action into rotation

Dipstick to check oil level

Sump is filled with oil to reduce friction

HOW A GAS ENGINE WORKS
Most engines use the four-stroke cycle, a four-cylinder engine fires twice per revolution. Each cylinder operates out of step with the others to give smoother running.

Piston

Connecting rod

Hot gases expand and force the piston down

Oil is pumped up into cylinders to lubricate pistons

Inlet valve *Piston* *Ignition system causes a spark* *Spark plug*

Crankshaft *Exhaust valve* *Exhaust valve*

1 INTAKE
As the piston is pulled downward by the crankshaft, the inlet valve is opened by a cam on the camshaft, and air is drawn in through an air filter. A carefully measured quantity of fuel is injected into the air stream under electronic control.

2 COMPRESSION
For the next half-revolution of the crankshaft, both valves are closed. The piston is pushed upward, compressing the fuel-air mixture. Just as the piston reaches the top, the ignition system puts a high voltage across the plug, causing a spark.

3 POWER
The spark ignites the mixture of fuel and air, which burns explosively, causing a rapid rise in temperature. It is at this point that heat energy is converted into mechanical energy: the piston is forced downward, turning the crankshaft.

4 EXHAUST
The exhaust valve opens, and the crankshaft, driven by energy stored in a heavy flywheel (and also by another cylinder in a multi-cylinder engine), pushes the piston up again. This pumps out the burned gases.

JAPANESE BULLET
Trains use much less energy than cars to move people around. Many modern trains are electric, but their power still comes from a heat engine, located in a generating station many miles away. This electric train, popularly known as the "Bullet," travels between Tokyo and Osaka on the Japanese Shinkansen high-speed rail network, which was set up in the early 1960s to provide a fast passenger service. Its top speed is 130 mph (210 km/h) and it runs on a specially built track. The French TGV (*train à grande vitesse*) is even faster, but needs an almost straight track. In Britain, trains run at over 125 mph (200 km/h) on ordinary tracks.

A JET ENGINE (below)

In a jet engine, fuel is mixed with air, compressed, burned, and exhausted in one smooth, continuous process. There are no pistons shuttling back and forth to slow it down. In the simplest type, the turbojet, all the mechanical work is done directly by the hot gases accelerating backward and so pushing the engine forward, as in a rocket. The turbofan, the type of engine now used on most passenger aircraft, has a large fan at the front that blows air around the outside of the engine. This air helps to propel the aircraft forward and also screens off the fast-moving stream of exhaust, making the engine more efficient and a lot quieter.

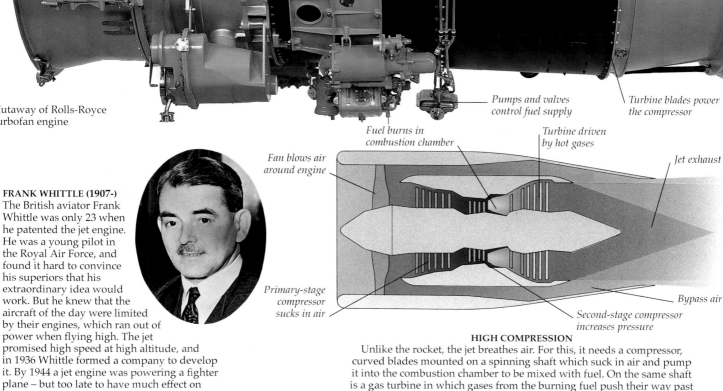

Compressor blades pump air into combustion chamber

Fuel-air mixture burns in combustion chamber

Fan blows bypass air through this space

Fan

Cutaway of Rolls-Royce turbofan engine

Pumps and valves control fuel supply

Turbine blades power the compressor

Fuel burns in combustion chamber

Fan blows air around engine

Turbine driven by hot gases

Jet exhaust

Primary-stage compressor sucks in air

Second-stage compressor increases pressure

Bypass air

FRANK WHITTLE (1907-)

The British aviator Frank Whittle was only 23 when he patented the jet engine. He was a young pilot in the Royal Air Force, and found it hard to convince his superiors that his extraordinary idea would work. But he knew that the aircraft of the day were limited by their engines, which ran out of power when flying high. The jet promised high speed at high altitude, and in 1936 Whittle formed a company to develop it. By 1944 a jet engine was powering a fighter plane – but too late to have much effect on the Second World War (1939-1945).

HIGH COMPRESSION

Unlike the rocket, the jet breathes air. For this, it needs a compressor, curved blades mounted on a spinning shaft which suck in air and pump it into the combustion chamber to be mixed with fuel. On the same shaft is a gas turbine in which gases from the burning fuel push their way past more blades, turning the shaft and so keeping the compressor going.

Mass production

Guide for moving mold part

MASS PRODUCTION ENGINEER
The American engineer Eli Whitney (1765-1825) was one of the first to make products – muskets for the American government – with parts so accurate that they were completely interchangeable.

THERE ARE TWO WAYS OF MAKING anything. One person can make the whole of it, or several people can each carry out one operation of the whole. The second way is mass production. Breaking manufacturing down into simple steps allows it to be done by machines or less skilled workers, and more quickly. Machines can be relied upon to repeat a simple operation endlessly without faltering, and workers repeating a simple task learn to work fast. But this kind of organization means that people never have the satisfaction of making a complete product, while engineers have to maintain high precision if all the parts are to fit together. As so often happens in technology, it was military pressure that created the need for improved techniques, when Eli Whitney was contracted to make 10,000 muskets to prepare the American army for a possible war with France. The parts had to be so accurate that any part would fit any musket.

A PAIR OF MOLDING DIES
This precision tool was designed with the help of a computer (p. 55) and handbuilt by skilled toolmakers. It can make 40 pump components (left) every hour. It is the people who craft these tools who actually create the shapes of familiar products made by the million – the rest of the system merely reproduces them.

MOLDED PUMP COMPONENT
Injection-molded plastics are ideal for mass production. Once the tools that shape the plastic have been made, the same part can be reproduced many thousands of times with excellent accuracy. Complex shapes can be molded by using tools with moving parts. Small shapes can be molded many at a time. Injection-molded parts can be recognized by a blemish where the plastic was injected (usually underneath, or covered by a label) and by "witness lines" which show where the several parts of the mold came together.

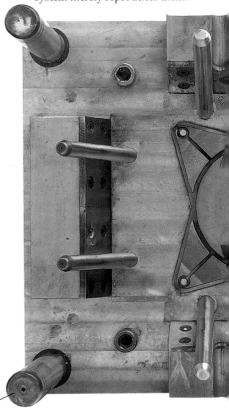

HOW INJECTION MOLDING WORKS
Plastic granules (p. 26) from the hopper are melted in the barrel and fed forward by the rotating screw. As pressure builds up at the nozzle, the screw is forced backward. When enough plastic has accumulated, the screw pushes quickly forward, pumping hot plastic into the cool mold, where it solidifies.

Locating rods guide mold halves together

Molded lettering

Nozzle

Granules fed through the hopper

The two halves of the mold press together and then pull apart

Screw rotates to feed the plastic toward the mold

Heater melts the granules

Hot plastic is injected into the mold

Locating rod

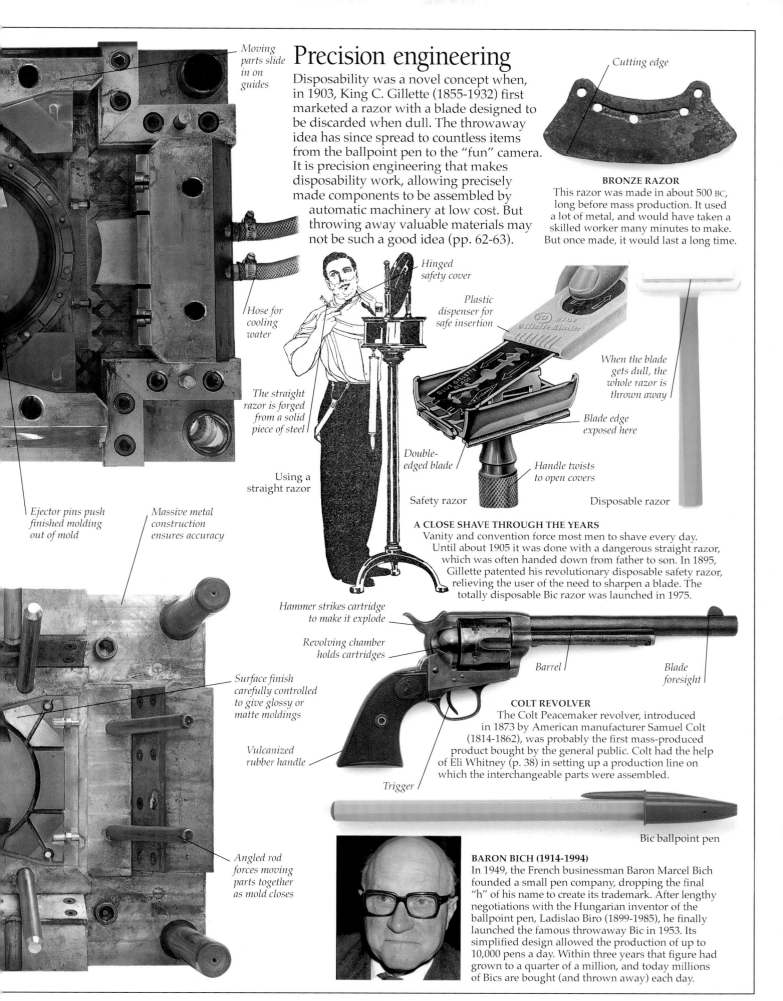

Precision engineering

Disposability was a novel concept when, in 1903, King C. Gillette (1855-1932) first marketed a razor with a blade designed to be discarded when dull. The throwaway idea has since spread to countless items from the ballpoint pen to the "fun" camera. It is precision engineering that makes disposability work, allowing precisely made components to be assembled by automatic machinery at low cost. But throwing away valuable materials may not be such a good idea (pp. 62-63).

Moving parts slide in on guides

Hose for cooling water

Ejector pins push finished molding out of mold

Massive metal construction ensures accuracy

The straight razor is forged from a solid piece of steel

Using a straight razor

Cutting edge

BRONZE RAZOR
This razor was made in about 500 BC, long before mass production. It used a lot of metal, and would have taken a skilled worker many minutes to make. But once made, it would last a long time.

Hinged safety cover

Plastic dispenser for safe insertion

When the blade gets dull, the whole razor is thrown away

Blade edge exposed here

Double-edged blade

Handle twists to open covers

Safety razor

Disposable razor

A CLOSE SHAVE THROUGH THE YEARS
Vanity and convention force most men to shave every day. Until about 1905 it was done with a dangerous straight razor, which was often handed down from father to son. In 1895, Gillette patented his revolutionary disposable safety razor, relieving the user of the need to sharpen a blade. The totally disposable Bic razor was launched in 1975.

Surface finish carefully controlled to give glossy or matte moldings

Vulcanized rubber handle

Hammer strikes cartridge to make it explode

Revolving chamber holds cartridges

Barrel

Blade foresight

Trigger

COLT REVOLVER
The Colt Peacemaker revolver, introduced in 1873 by American manufacturer Samuel Colt (1814-1862), was probably the first mass-produced product bought by the general public. Colt had the help of Eli Whitney (p. 38) in setting up a production line on which the interchangeable parts were assembled.

Angled rod forces moving parts together as mold closes

Bic ballpoint pen

BARON BICH (1914-1994)
In 1949, the French businessman Baron Marcel Bich founded a small pen company, dropping the final "h" of his name to create its trademark. After lengthy negotiations with the Hungarian inventor of the ballpoint pen, Ladislao Biro (1899-1985), he finally launched the famous throwaway Bic in 1953. Its simplified design allowed the production of up to 10,000 pens a day. Within three years that figure had grown to a quarter of a million, and today millions of Bics are bought (and thrown away) each day.

Domestic lives

EARLY DISHWASHER
After heating the water herself, this domestic servant had to wash the dishes without the benefit of modern detergents.

WHEN TECHNOLOGY CREATED clothing for people to wear and shelters for them to live in, it also created a never-ending need to look after these things. Cleaning, cooking, mending, making fires, and trimming lamp wicks were all new tasks, and in most societies it was women who undertook these jobs. Although this is slowly changing, the pattern persists today. Machines now do many of the backbreaking jobs like sweeping and washing, but standards of hygiene have risen, too, leaving many people with just as much domestic work to do. Two big advances improved modern domestic life – 19th-century sewage systems that allowed cities to grow without the risk of disease, and early 20th-century electric power that made good lighting and domestic machinery possible. Domestic life has also been improved by new materials like plastics (pp. 26-27).

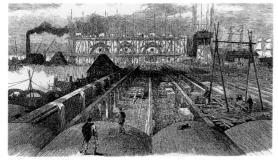

SEWAGE WORKS
People cannot live in cities without technology. Three epidemics of cholera killed over 20,000 people in London between 1832 and 1854. They caught the disease by drinking water containing sewage that had been dumped in the River Thames. In 1858, work was started on huge pipes that would take the effluent toward the mouth of the river, where the tides could wash it out to sea. The project was completed by 1875. It involved draining 24 sq miles (60 sq km) of marshland and building two giant pumping stations, one seen here under construction.

BELLOWS VACUUM CLEANER
This early 20th-century vacuum cleaner took two people to work it – one to pump the bellows, and one to steer. By the 1930s, with the building of power stations and networks of cables, many homes had electric power. Electric vacuum cleaners became possible, but without modern materials such as plastics, they remained heavy, clumsy, and expensive.

Bellows pump in air

Dirt sucked in through the hose

CYCLONE ACTION
Versatile modern materials have now made it possible to adapt powerful industrial machinery for use in the home. The cyclone cleaner is part vacuum cleaner, part tornado. Dirt is dislodged and sucked in by a powerful current of air. Instead of passing through a porous bag, the air is forced to spin at high speed, whirling the dust with it. In an inner, conical chamber, the air is slowed down so that it drops the dust into a bin which, unlike a vacuum cleaner bag, cannot clog.

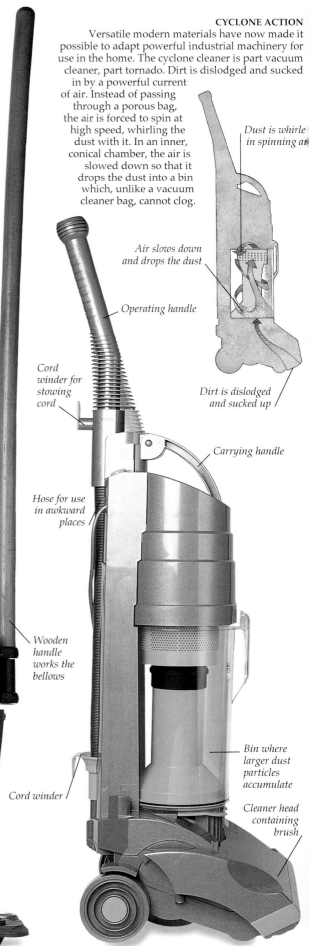

Dust is whirle in spinning ai

Air slows down and drops the dust

Operating handle

Cord winder for stowing cord

Hose for use in awkward places

Carrying handle

Wooden handle works the bellows

Cord winder

Bin where larger dust particles accumulate

Cleaner head containing brush

Lighting the home

Gas and oil were used for lighting homes in the 19th century. Both were dim and dangerous. As soon as inventors had solved the problem of making an electric filament white-hot without it burning away, other light sources were consigned to history. The first electric lamps had carbon filaments in a vacuum, but by 1913, lightbulbs had brighter metal filaments and were also filled with inert gas to prevent the filament from boiling away and spreading itself over the glass.

Electric heating wires inside panels

Ornamentation influenced by the Arts and Crafts movement of the 1890s

Wick is continually burned away, keeping it the right length

BURNING A CANDLE
Very little of the energy trapped in candle wax emerges as light. Nevertheless, a modern candle is a highly developed piece of technology. The wax and wick are perfectly matched so that the entire candle burns away without dripping or leaving any unburned wax.

Cloth wick feeds oil to flame

Glass prevents flame from blowing out

KEROSENE LAMP
Oil lamps replaced candles as soon as there was a suitable oil to put in them. This lamp uses kerosene, a light oil produced by distilling petroleum, which was discovered in the US around 1860.

Oil reservoir

Sheet steel body

Screw base designed by Edison

Switch controls heating elements

EDISON LIGHTBULB
Thomas Edison (1847-1931) in the US and Joseph Swan (1828-1914) in Britain both produced lightbulbs in the same year, 1879. Their bulbs were on sale by 1881. The filament was made of carbon, and air was pumped out of the bulb to prevent the carbon from burning. The bulbs were not very bright, but they were a great improvement on anything else at the time.

Carbon filament made from bamboo

Plastic cover conceals metal base

MODERN LIGHTBULB
This modern incandescent lightbulb lasts over twice as long and gives four times as much light as Edison's early offering (left). The metal used for the filament is tungsten, which melts at a higher temperature than any other. The bulb is filled with the inert gas argon, produced by distilling liquefied air. The filament is coiled and then coiled again, to concentrate its heat and increase efficiency.

High vacuum within bulb

"Pip" where air was sucked out

Bulb filled with argon gas

Coiled tungsten filament

AN ELECTRIC IMITATION
Domestic life was turned upside down between 1900 and 1930. Servants almost disappeared, to be replaced by electrical gadgets of all kinds. It was too much for some people, who wanted their new appliances to look as much like the old ones as possible. So although this early electric heater needs no one to stoke it, it is made to look like an old-fashioned stove.

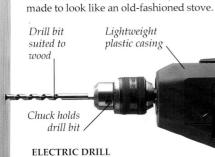

Drill bit suited to wood

Lightweight plastic casing

Chuck holds drill bit

ELECTRIC DRILL
The first portable electric drill was made in 1917. It weighed 24 lb (11 kg). This modern drill weighs 3.5 lb (1.5 kg). Modern materials – better iron and insulation for its motor, and a rugged, lightweight plastic casing – have made it possible. More recently, improved battery technology has made cordless drills practical. Although the electric drill burns up valuable fuel with every hole it makes, many people see it as an indispensable part of do-it-yourself. People with such tools can work much faster, tackling building jobs in their spare time instead of paying someone else to do it.

COMPACT FLUORESCENT LAMP
A fluorescent lamp works in a different way from an ordinary lightbulb. An electrical discharge through mercury vapor emits ultraviolet light, which makes a coating inside the tube glow brightly. This gives about four times as much light as an ordinary bulb of the same wattage. In its usual form the lamp needs heavy starting gear and is long and clumsy, but by using electronics to raise the electrical frequency (the number of voltage reversals per second) from around 50 to around 50,000, everything can be made much smaller. With the tube folded up to fit into existing light fixtures, homes can be lit at a fraction of the normal cost.

Folded fluorescent tube

Electronics in base

Fits ordinary bulb holder

Ordinary bulb would take over three times the current

The technology of the car

IN ITS SHAPE, THE CAR has changed little in the 100 years since the first gas-powered "horseless carriages" rumbled uncertainly onto roads built to take horse-drawn vehicles. Mechanically, the car is improving all the time. To make a functional car, a light, portable power source is needed. At first, steam engines and electric motors were used, but neither was quite suitable: the steam engine was too heavy and slow to start, and the electric motor was burdened with massive batteries. It was the internal combustion engine (p. 36) – so called because the fuel burns inside it, not outside as with a steam engine – that really got the automobile revolution started. Since then, development has been gradual but continuous, with each year seeing new, improved models, more vehicles on the roads, and more roads to take them. Densely populated countries are now starting to run out of space, and the fuel source will soon run out. There are safety problems, too, because accidents involving cars kill tens of thousands of people each year.

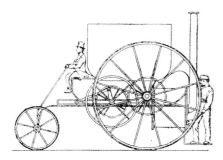

STEAM CARRIAGE
Steam engines, running on railroad tracks, were transporting people and goods 50 years before the car. By the 1850s, with advances in materials and better understanding of scientific principles, it was possible to make steam-powered road vehicles.

HENRY FORD (1863-1947)
Henry Ford was the American engineer who, in 1908, revolutionized personal transportation with his Model T, the first car that ordinary people could afford. He was not the first to produce cars on an assembly line, where each worker performs the same operation on each car – this was introduced by Fiat in 1912. But his policy of simple designs and constant price reductions quickly made his company a world leader. Ford is seen here in the sort of car his methods made obsolete.

THE MODERN SEDAN CAR
Japanese car manufacturer Toyota entered the luxury car market with the Lexus in 1992. The basic layout of engine, transmission, and passenger and luggage compartments was well established 70 years ago. The difference lies in the details and the increasing use of electronic technology. The engine and many other systems are under electronic control, while the automatic transmission makes driving easy.

Careful design of seating and controls, together with low noise levels, reduces fatigue on long journeys

Heated rear window

Noise insulation

Urethane paint resists chipping

Bumper returns to its original shape after low-speed impacts

Coil spring suspension

Stainless-steel exhaust system fitted with a catalytic converter to clean up emissions

Gas-filled shock absorbers

Magnesium-alloy wheel

Straight driveshaft minimizes vibration

THE CONCEPT IN WOOD

Designers have been playing around with the possible permutations of engine, wheels, and seats ever since the first cars appeared. Several full-scale models are always built during the planning stage of any new car, usually from clay over a wooden frame, so that the design can be evaluated and refined. The French architect Le Corbusier (1887-1965) came up with this odd-looking arrangement in the 1920s. Le Corbusier's car never got beyond the wooden mock-up stage, although it has a passing resemblance to the Citroen 2CV, a hugely popular car in France until it ceased production in the 1980s.

Engine and luggage compartment

Large windshield

Car is propelled forward on a track

Dummy

Safety airbag inflates

Crumple zone absorbs energy

Solid concrete wall

ENSURING SAFETY STANDARDS

Unfortunately, cars do crash, and engineers try to minimize the effects. Having installed seat belts, the next step is to ensure that a crashing car slows down as slowly as possible. Front and rear "crumple zones" are designed to absorb lethal energy by buckling in a crash. A test rig is used to check that the design works as planned.

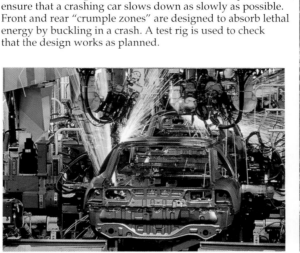

CAR-MAKING ROBOTS

Early cars were built on a heavy frame, the chassis. In the late 1920s the self-supporting steel monocoque body was developed. Steel panels are pressed to shape (p. 11) and then joined together to form a strong, light shell that supports engine, wheels, and seats. Robots do the hot, repetitive job of welding car bodies. The panels to be joined are clamped together while a heavy electric current is passed through them, melting the two sheets of metal into one.

THE DEMANDS OF TRAFFIC

Cars get us and our belongings around fast and flexibly, beating all other forms of transport for sheer convenience. But their success may be their downfall. Pollution and accidents take lives, and the increasing need for space is forcing planners to destroy communities by driving multilane highways right through them.

Laminated glass sunroof

Electric window

Heated rear-view mirror

Steering column

Electronic dashboard

Central locking and security system

Safety airbags inflate on impact to protect the driver and passenger

On-board computer controls fuel injection and ignition

Computer-controlled anti-lock braking system

Radial-ply tires

Lightweight aluminum radiator

4.0 liter V8 engine is made largely from aluminum alloy (p. 15)

Farming

AGRICULTURE IN THE 13TH CENTURY
This medieval illustration shows what farming was like around the 13th century. After plowing, seed was broadcast – simply scattered on the ground. What survived and grew was later harvested with simple hand tools like the sickle. There were no fertilizers, but each strip of land was allowed to lie fallow, or unused, for one year in three to regain its fertility.

WHEN PEOPLE STARTED FARMING about 10,000 years ago, it was their first major attempt to take control of the environment. Before then they found food wherever they could. Farming takes less time than gathering plants or hunting, and so releases people to do other work, including the development of machines and methods to improve farming itself. Farming technology has developed alongside industry. After the plow, it changed little until the 18th century, when workers began to leave the land for better wages in the new factories (pp. 34-35). Developments like the seed drill and fertilizers made it possible to farm with fewer people and get higher yields. In some places this has led to overproduction. Elsewhere, though, these changes have passed farmers by, and they must often depend on the surplus produce of richer nations to survive.

The handles are used to steer the plow

Large blades mark soil for lining up the next row

Large wheel turns a roller inside the drill, pushing out the seeds

THREE ACTIONS IN ONE
The plow was developed about 4,000 years ago and has been an important farming implement ever since. Its job is to turn over the top layer of the soil. This does three useful things: it digs in the stubble of the last crop; it exposes the soil to the weather to improve its texture; and it buries weeds so that they die. Modern plows, drawn by tractors, can cut several furrows at once.

Harness link to attach to the horse or ox

The coulter makes the first cut of the soil

The moldboard turns the loosened soil over to form a furrow

The share breaks up the soil

Wooden handle

Rivet

Cutting edge

HAND SCYTHE
Hand tools have not entirely disappeared from farming. This modern hand scythe, made in a factory from hardened steel sheet rivetted to ordinary steel rod, is the descendant of earlier tools like the sickle which would have been forged in one piece by a blacksmith. Its curved blade makes it ideal for trimming hedges and other small cutting jobs.

EFFICIENT SHEEP FARMING
Sheep were introduced into Australia for their wool. The wool was exported all over the world, but the perishable meat had to be eaten locally. This left many surplus carcasses, which were either burned or else boiled down to make soap in factories like this, pictured in 1868. The technology of refrigeration, developed in the late 19th century (p. 46), meant that meat could be transported long distances to where it was needed.

BREWING AND BREEDING
Farming methods led to modern biotechnology (pp. 60-61). Brewing uses microorganisms to turn grain into beer, while animal breeding has helped in the study of genetics.

Handles to
steer drill

Hopper lid

Seeds are
poured in here

Hopper

Small wheels take the
weight of the drill

GRAIN MOUNTAIN
Sun, rain, and air provide nearly all a plant
needs to grow. But one vital substance, nitrogen,
although abundant in the air, can come only
from the soil. Lack of nitrogen in the soil is what
limits the growth of most crops. In the late 19th
century, chemicals containing nitrogen began to
be applied to the land, producing spectacular
increases in yield. When used with other
techniques, such as spraying crops to kill
weeds, fertilizers can lead to overproduction.
The unwanted produce can be stored, as this
grain has been, but this is expensive.

Blade makes a groove
for seeds to lie in

Model of a drill (1828)

SEED DRILL
Much precious seed was wasted or eaten by birds
when it was sown by hand. The seed drill, introduced by
the English farmer Jethro Tull (1674-1741) in 1701, was a great
improvement. It distributed the seeds evenly, so that plants grew
better and weeding was easier; it buried them, so that birds were
denied a meal; and it was much quicker. The seeds in this 1828
drill were drawn out of the wooden hopper by rollers driven
by the large wheel, ensuring even distribution at all speeds.

Horse's harness
is attached here

Shaft

The elevator takes
the wheat into the
mechanism

The stalks are separated
from the ears

The ears pass
into the thresher

The grain
is extracted

The reel forces
the wheat on to
the cutter bar

Cutter bar

Unwanted
chaff

HARVESTING FACTORY
The combine harvester was developed in the US, where enormous mid-
western fields needed advanced machinery to gather the grain. It is an
automatic, mobile factory, allowing two workers to harvest and process
the crop. The plants are cut, the part containing the grain separated from
the stalk, and the grain threshed, or beaten, to separate it from the
unwanted material, or chaff. The clean grain is pumped into an
attendant truck, while the stalks become useful bundles of straw
that can be dumped for later collection.

HOW A COMBINE WORKS
The revolving reel forces the plants on to the cutter bar. They are lifted into
the mechanism by an elevator. The stalks are separated and bundled into
bales of straw, while the ears pass into the thresher. This extracts the grain
and blows away the chaff. The finished grain is propelled upward through
a pipe for delivery into a truck. Advanced models feature satellite and
computer technology that can analyze the yield of each field.

Taste and smell

TASTE AND SMELL ARE OUR FIRST LINE OF DEFENSE against poisoning and disease. Smell also tells us about our environment and can stir our feelings strongly, either attracting or repelling us. Flavors and aromas are now big business, with chemists able to imitate many of them. An important cause of unpleasant odors is food spoilage by bacteria, microscopic organisms that live and grow almost everywhere. Salting and pickling have been used for centuries to prevent the growth of bacteria, but make food taste different. Modern methods such as canning and freezing extend the life of foods while keeping more of their original flavor.

REFRIGERATED CARGO
In 1881, a batch of sheep carcasses reached England from New Zealand. The meat was in perfect condition. It had been kept frozen by one of the first refrigeration units on a ship.

The first commercial breakfast cereal

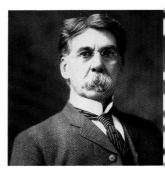

HENRY PERKY (1843-1906)
Perky was an American lawyer who suffered from chronic indigestion. In 1892 he invented a process for making wheat more digestible. The wheat grains were boiled, shredded, shaped into biscuits, and toasted, forming a food which became known as Shredded Wheat(TM).

MAKING FRESH CHEESE
Milk consists of fat and protein globules suspended in water. These can be made to stick together to form a solid curd so that the watery part, or whey, can be removed. The result is cheese. The curd forms when bacteria acidify the milk, or when milk is affected by rennet, an extract from the stomachs of calves. Fresh cheese has a high water content and cannot be stored for long.

Curds are poured into muslin

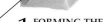

Muslin has a close weave and is ideal as a sieve

1 FORMING THE CURD
The milk is warmed to a temperature of about 86°F (30°C) and a small quantity of starter – milk containing suitable bacteria – is added. The bacteria feed on the natural sugar in the milk and turn it into acid. Rennet is added to hasten the formation of the curd. The curd and whey are poured into a piece of muslin in a colander.

2 SEPARATING THE WHEY
The curd contains a lot of trapped whey. This must be allowed to escape through the muslin so that the cheese becomes more solid. The use of high- or low-fat milk, slight changes in the temperature of the milk, and the use of animal or vegetable rennet all have an effect on the flavor and texture of the finished product. Soft unripened cheeses can be molded for a cheese board or used in cooking.

Cheese is hung in a cool place

Whey drips

Curd is covered with muslin

As the whey drains out, the curds thicken into cheese

3 WRAPPED IN MUSLIN
The muslin is folded into a bag. The whey that drains out is a useful food supplement that some cheese producers feed back to their cows. Over 80 percent of milk is water. A cheese intended to be ripened would have more water removed by pressing and be left for many weeks to develop flavor. Soft cheeses such as this are not designed to mature.

Colander

4 THE FINAL STAGE
The wet curd in its muslin bag is hung up and left to drip for several hours, forming the final, much drier product. It is then ready to be transferred into small containers for sale as *fromage frais* or *fromage blanc* (fresh or white cheese).

NICOLAS APPERT (1749-1841)
Appert was a French cook who developed a form of canning in 1824. It was the first process to preserve foods without drying them or spoiling their flavor with chemicals.

Macaroni and cheese

Chocolate pudding

SPACE FOOD
Feeding people in space is difficult. Since there is no gravity to keep things on a plate, droplets or crumbs would float around forever, so everything has to be packaged for direct transfer into the mouth. Because weight has to be kept as low as possible, foods are dehydrated, usually by freeze-drying. Water generated by the on-board electrical system is added to make the food edible. Freeze-drying food removes three-quarters of its weight. The food is first frozen, then air is pumped away to create a vacuum. Under these conditions the water in the food escapes as vapor, without first becoming liquid. The low temperature and absence of liquid water during drying mean that foods keep their nutrients, flavor, and texture.

Bread cubes

Tomato soup

PASTA MACHINE
Bacteria cannot multiply without water, so drying is an effective method of food preservation. Pasta, a paste of high-protein durum wheat flour, was invented in Italy, probably around the Middle Ages. The wheat is ground into a coarse flour known as semolina, then mixed with water and dried. In this form it can be stored for years, ready to be revived with boiling water when needed. Pasta can also be formed into shapes filled with cheese, meat, or vegetables and eaten fresh.

FREEZE-DRIED COFFEE
Granular instant coffee is made by freeze-drying the concentrated liquid from a giant brew of black coffee.

Sense of smell

Smell can create likes and dislikes, revive memories, and stir feelings like nothing else can. Technology can now work on this potent sense. Chemists are able to produce synthetic smells to mimic nature, and instruments are able to analyze and measure smells so that pleasant ones can be imitated and nasty ones eliminated.

AROMATHERAPY
Certain smells make us feel good, while others do the opposite. Aromatherapists study smells and have evolved a system which matches the powerful effects of natural aromas with the relief of certain conditions. Aromatherapy oils are extracted mostly from herbs and flowers.

Frankincense Jasmine Rose Lemon grass Chamomile

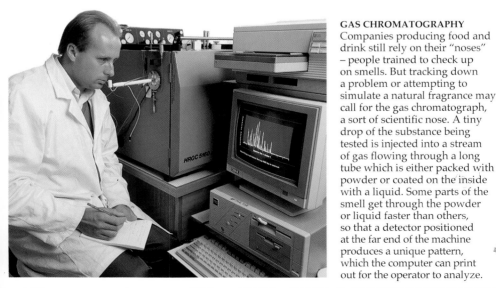

GAS CHROMATOGRAPHY
Companies producing food and drink still rely on their "noses" – people trained to check up on smells. But tracking down a problem or attempting to simulate a natural fragrance may call for the gas chromatograph, a sort of scientific nose. A tiny drop of the substance being tested is injected into a stream of gas flowing through a long tube which is either packed with powder or coated on the inside with a liquid. Some parts of the smell get through the powder or liquid faster than others, so that a detector positioned at the far end of the machine produces a unique pattern, which the computer can print out for the operator to analyze.

Mentha piperita (peppermint)

CLEAN AROMAS
Many strongly aromatic substances are oils. Familiar smells such as peppermint and spearmint come from oils produced by the genus (plant group) *Mentha*. Minty smells and tastes are associated with cleanliness, which is why synthetic mint essences go into everything from toothpaste to supermarket air-conditioning systems.

Personal communication

COMMUNICATION IS ONE OF OUR GREATEST SKILLS, yet without technology, it remains limited. Speech will reach only a short distance, and memory is unreliable. The invention of writing about 6,000 years ago allowed messages to be sent long distances and stored forever. In the 15th century, printing brought these benefits to a wider public. But it was the application of electricity to communication in the 19th century that revolutionized the pace and scale of our lives, shrinking the time required to send messages from weeks to seconds and eventually allowing people to talk from continent to continent. Development has been rapid and continuous. It is hard to believe that 60 years ago there was no television and few international telephone links.

MEDIEVAL SCRIBE
Until about 1455, when German goldsmith Johannes Gutenberg (c. 1400-1468) perfected a way of printing books cheaply, the only way to copy a book was for a scribe to create the copy by hand.

A trimmed goose feather

NATURAL COMMUNICATION
Plants give out simple visual signals to ensure their survival. The flower attracts the insect with its shape, scent, and color, and the insect obliges by pollinating it and other flowers.

A penknife was used to trim the pointed end

THE QUILL PEN
Until metal pen nibs appeared, people wrote with feathers. A large wing feather from a goose was the usual choice. The feather was trimmed and the end of the quill, or shaft, was cut to a pointed shape with a penknife. Alternatively, a specially designed cutter would clip the end to shape in a single movement. A slit in the end of the quill fed ink to the paper, while the hollow shaft held enough ink for a few words of writing.

WAITING FOR THE TECHNOLOGY
A good idea often has to wait a long time for the technologies that will make it a reality. The basic principle of fax (short for facsimile, a perfect copy) was worked out by Scottish inventor Alexander Bain (1810-1877) in 1843, but without electronics (pp. 54-55), it was too slow to be useful. It was the microchip that finally boosted Bain's idea. The modern fax uses a computer on a chip to convert images into codes that can be sent quickly and reliably over ordinary telephone lines.

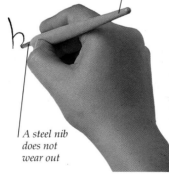

Wooden pen holder

THE DIP PEN
Cheap steel meant pen nibs were common by the end of the 19th century. It proved surprisingly difficult to imitate the smooth action of the goose quill, and many different nibs were tried. A small cup in the nib sometimes held an ink reserve, replacing the hollow quill, but the actual writing point was usually just a copy of the trimmed feather that had been used for centuries. Steel nibs did not wear out, so the penknife soon lost its original purpose.

A steel nib does not wear out

Fiber tip

THE FELT-TIP PEN
The felt-tip pen originated in Japan in the 1960s. It is based on the writing brushes used in the East for centuries, but modern plastics are used to turn this traditional instrument into a self-contained tool. Ink is held in nylon fibers which feed it to the tip by capillary action – the ink is attracted to the narrow fibers and so drawn along the spaces between them. The design has now been adapted for many different inks and writing points.

A fax is sent over an ordinary phone line

Japanese language uses too many characters for a teleprinter, but the fax can handle any number

Ink supply is held in fibers inside body

Worldwide network

The dream of distant speech was realized by Scottish teacher Alexander Graham Bell (1847-1922) in 1876 with the invention of the telephone. (American Elisha Gray (1835-1901) tried to register a similar patent two hours later.) Bell Laboratories developed the mobile telephone in 1979, and now someone standing in a street can chat with a friend on another continent. The networks that make this possible depend on computers, which can also exchange images and data of all kinds. A computer and a telephone line can now access systems like Internet, a network of networks that has become a meeting place and information source for people all over the world. Commercial networks can provide financial services, entertainment, medical advice, armchair shopping, and learning for those living in remote areas.

Earpiece

Aerial sends and receives radio signals

Keys like those on an ordinary telephone

The entire telephone fits in the palm of the hand

Digital display shows the stage that the communication has reached

Microphone folds back when not in use

EARLY TELEPHONE EXCHANGE
Technology often relies on other technological breakthroughs. If American undertaker Almon B. Strowger (1839-1902) had not invented the automatic exchange in 1889, the increasing cost of connecting telephone calls would eventually have strangled the system. An operator was needed to connect every call by plugging a wire into a switchboard. The first automatic exchanges were noisy mechanical monsters, but now the job is done silently by computers. People are still needed to deal with problems the machines cannot handle.

CELLULAR TELEPHONE
Twenty years ago this tiny communication device was science fiction. Now it is almost taken for granted. It was made possible by many technologies coming together: plastics (pp. 26-27), improved radio techniques, better batteries, computers, and above all the microchip (p. 54). An array of low-powered radio stations links the moving telephone to a computer network that keeps track of where the telephone is. To avoid interference, neighboring radio stations use different frequencies, but the credit-card-sized telephone is able to tune instantly from one frequency to another, maintaining continuous contact between users.

Communication fed in here when sending a fax

Paper stored inside for receiving messages

VIDEO CONFERENCING
The idea of a device that lets you see a distant person, as well as hear what is said, has been around for almost as long as the telephone. But, as with fax, it needed computers and microchips to make it work. The problem is that pictures contain a lot of information, much of it of little use, which makes them expensive to send by wire. Computers can now compress pictures for cheaper transmission, allowing people to confer in groups over vast distances – a video conference – instead of meeting face to face. The experimental setup here could soon be available worldwide.

Using color

THE HUMAN SENSE OF COLOR may have developed because it helped our distant ancestors to pick out ripe fruit. Color can still make us feel happy or sad, and it literally "colors our judgement" when we choose between rival products, so designers and manufacturers take color seriously. Technology can help in several ways. Better dyes now offer purer clothing colors that do not fade, while new pigments give cleaner, stronger shades to cars and cosmetics. Color can now be measured accurately, replacing unreliable judgements with recorded figures so that products stay the same from batch to batch. These standard measurements (pp. 30-31) enable components made on opposite sides of the globe to match when they come together. And now that electronics and computers can splash fashionable shades on screens, magazines, and posters everywhere, our awareness of color is greater than ever.

EARLY DYE WORKS
Until 1856, when William Perkin (1838-1907) accidentally made the first synthetic dye, cloth was colored with dyes extracted from plants or animals. Some blue denim is still colored with the vegetable dye indigo. Most other natural dyes have been replaced by synthetics made from coal or oil, which are cheaper, easier to use, and do not run or fade.

The figures are recorded for comparison with data from other batches

Reference number is recognized internationally

The colorimeter is held over a mustard sample

Electronic sensors respond to the reflected light to give a reading

COLOR MATCHING
Consumers are color-conscious about food products. The slightest deviation from the expected color will cause buyers to look elsewhere. This is a problem for manufacturers, because products made from natural ingredients are likely to vary in color from batch to batch. The product's color is controlled by blending ingredients from different sources. By taking readings of each batch on an accurately calibrated colorimeter, food technologists can ensure consistent color every time.

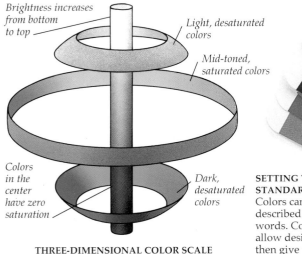

Brightness increases from bottom to top

Light, desaturated colors

Mid-toned, saturated colors

Colors in the center have zero saturation

Dark, desaturated colors

THREE-DIMENSIONAL COLOR SCALE
Colors can be classified by hue, saturation, and brightness. Hue corresponds to position in the spectrum (p. 58). Saturation refers to strength, and brightness describes color as seen in a black-and-white picture. A three-dimensional sphere can show how colors are related.

SETTING THE STANDARD
Colors cannot be described precisely in words. Color-matching systems allow designers to choose colors and then give printers or other suppliers a reference number or sample that tells them exactly what is required. The systems work by mixing a limited number of basic pigments in different proportions to give a wide range of colors. Matching systems are used worldwide to provide practical standards for printing, packaging, and product design.

Black from soot

Verona green dug
from earth

Yellow ochre dug
from earth

Red ochre dug
from earth

Ultramarine blue from
lapis lazuli stone

Egyptian blue,
containing silicon,
copper, and calcium

NATURAL COLORS

Dyes and pigments both provide color, but in different ways. Dyes can dissolve in a liquid, and they attach themselves to a material as separate molecules. Pigments, like the ancient colors shown here, are simply tiny fragments of a colored substance that can be stuck onto surfaces in the form of paint, or mixed into plastics to color them all the way through (p. 26). Some pigments are obtained by grinding up rocks and are therefore permanent.

ACRYLIC COLORS

Acrylic paints consist of minute droplets of acrylic (pp. 26-27) suspended in water with pigments. They can be diluted with water. When the water evaporates, the droplets join up to form a waterproof coating.

Red acrylic   Yellow acrylic

A PROTECTIVE COATING

Oil paint was developed in the 15th century. It was originally made with linseed oil, the oil of the flax plant, boiled and diluted with turpentine. Linseed oil reacts with oxygen in the air to form a tough coating. Modern paints are made with synthetic resins derived from petroleum. The color of paint comes from millions of tiny particles of pigment, each of which absorbs some colors and reflects others. Oil paint is not merely decorative; for this iron anchor chain, the paint is also needed to protect the metal from air and water, and so from rust.

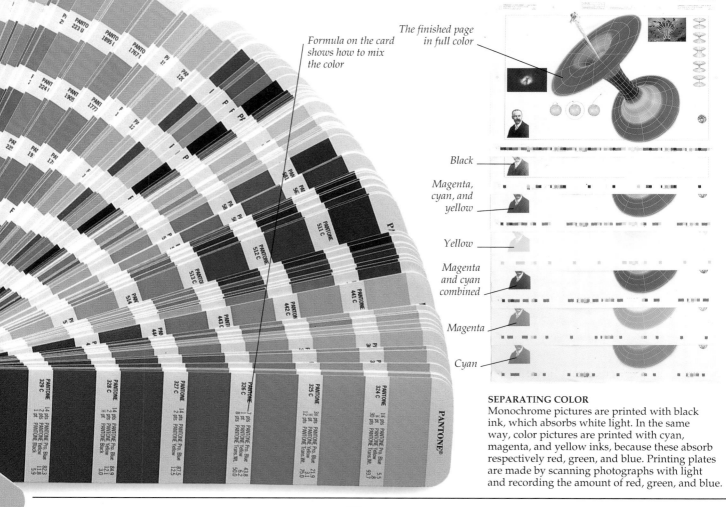

Formula on the card
shows how to mix
the color

The finished page
in full color

Black

Magenta,
cyan, and
yellow

Yellow

Magenta
and cyan
combined

Magenta

Cyan

SEPARATING COLOR

Monochrome pictures are printed with black ink, which absorbs white light. In the same way, color pictures are printed with cyan, magenta, and yellow inks, because these absorb respectively red, green, and blue. Printing plates are made by scanning photographs with light and recording the amount of red, green, and blue.

Concept and design

INVENTORS HIT ON A NEW PRINCIPLE and then look for problems it will solve. Designers start with a problem and look for solutions based on principles they already know. There is a fine line between invention and design: many designers do invent new products, while some who claim to be inventors are merely recycling old ideas. Engineering designers use largely scientific techniques to work out how to build bridges, cars, or computers. Industrial designers concentrate on incorporating elegance, convenience, and human appeal. Fashion designers use flair and market knowledge to specify products that will have a short but intense life. Most designers work as part of a team, each member specializing in a different aspect of the job, and all designers work within strict limits of time and cost.

19TH-CENTURY KITCHEN
Good design reflects the needs of the time. Today's smaller, more convenient kitchens are designed for families without servants.

Logo

Cast-iron body

Speed control

Stainless steel bowl with glossy finish

INDUSTRIAL LOOKS
Food machinery spread from the factory into domestic kitchens in the 1940s in the US, and in the 1950s in Europe. This 1950s mixer shows its industrial origins in the cast-iron and stainless-steel construction and the technical-looking controls. The only concessions to domesticity are size, a coat of red paint, and a flashy logo. Some people prefer industrial-looking domestic appliances for their classic honesty and sturdy construction.

Catch releases attachments

Stirring mechanism spins blades and moves them around the bowl

The beater is designed so that the whole area of the bowl is covered

Die-cast alloy body

Stainless steel bowl with brushed finish

Smooth exterior for easy cleaning

Hinge for lifting mixer arm is concealed inside body

MODERN MIXER
In the 1950s, the industrial designer was often called upon only to add some styling to a product that had already been designed. This led to unattractive products that cost more than they should have. By the 1960s designers had learned more about engineering, and engineers had started to think about how people see and use products. The resulting partnership has increased the appeal of mass-produced products of all kinds. This food mixer, made in 1992 by the same company as the one above, has a smoother, lighter die-cast alloy body (pp. 16-17). It is easier and safer to use and clean, and incorporates a more powerful motor with electronic speed control.

JOHN SMEATON (1724-1792)

British engineer John Smeaton was perhaps the first professional designer. He specialized in problem solving. Asked for a new lighthouse, he produced a successful design based on the shape of a tree.

Traditional 19th-century building

Steel frame

REALTY BUILDING, CHICAGO

When steel for high-rise buildings began to be available in the late 19th century, American architects and engineers gladly seized on it as a solution to packing more people on to a crowded site. But the designer of this building of 1898, recognizing that people were used to buildings with stone walls, clothed the steel frame in ornate cladding. The buildings of the Modern Movement of the 1930s were the first in which the true structure was allowed to show.

ARCHITECTURAL MODEL

Many designers deal with complex systems. Architects and town planners sometimes have the almost impossible task of working out how people will live in a totally new environment. Models like this are made to convey the planner's concepts to a client. Living systems are unpredictable, and usually take many years of trial and adjustment to get right.

Landscape feature
Hospital buildings

Model of a hospital complex

WIND-TUNNEL TESTING

Customers today want faster cars, but they also expect lower fuel consumption. So aerodynamic drag, the resistance of the air to a car going through it, has become important. The airflow over a newly designed car can be checked using smoke in a wind tunnel. If a curve suggested by the stylists gets in the way of the air, it may have to change.

Engine

JET TEST

A big jet engine is complex and powerful, so to test a new design straight off the drawing board, elaborate arrangements are made. There is always the possibility that some unexpected effect may show up – engineers are learning all the time. The engine here is supported on a test rig in the open air so that noise levels can be measured by a battery of microphones. Radio signals (radiometry) carry messages back to a computer. These will give a wealth of computerized data about speed, temperature, noise, and vibration to help the engineers spot any faults and make corrections.

COMPUTER-AIDED DESIGN

It is impossible now to imagine design without computers. Engineers of 30 years ago worked without even a pocket calculator. Many problems could not be solved, because the necessary mathematics would have taken too long. Engineering designers now use powerful work stations that can visualize their creations in color and three dimensions. Simply checking that all the parts will fit together without bumping into each other saves an enormous amount of time. For really difficult problems, like designing the best shapes for the flow of fluids, the computer is indispensable. Once the product is designed, the specifications can go, via computer, directly to the shop floor for manufacturing.

Two-dimensional diagram showing the connections in a network

Three-dimensional model of a complex assembly showing how parts fit

Electronics and computing

ELECTRONICS IS A RELATIVELY NEW TECHNOLOGY. Transistors, the key components of microchips, were invented in 1947. Microchips themselves, which make modern electronic technology possible, did not appear until 1962. The key to electronics is the way it uses electricity to control more electricity. An electronic switch, unlike an ordinary light switch, can be operated by another electronic switch. Because of this, huge assemblies of switches – transistors – can be built up on a single chip and made to control each other, performing complex sequences of operations that transform one pattern of electricity into another. The rate of development of electronics, which feeds on itself as computers are used to design better computers, has been amazing. Computers now do thousands of times more than they could 50 years ago.

ALTERING SILICON TO MAKE CHIPS
Electronic chips are made by adding impurities to pure silicon, subtly altering it to produce microscopic patterns that control the flow of electricity. Here, an engineer checks on a vacuum chamber used for the production process.

Glass tube with metal parts in a vacuum

THE FIRST TUBES
In 1904 it was discovered that tiny particles called electrons, released by hot wires and traveling through a vacuum, could be used in an electric circuit. In 1906 the American Lee De Forest (1873-1961) found a way to control these electrons electrically, creating the first electronic device, the tube.

1950s tube

Metal tab to get rid of heat

THE TRANSISTOR
Like tubes, transistors work by controlling electrons, but the particles move through a solid, not a vacuum, and need no heat to release them. This makes transistors cheaper and smaller. Individual transistors like this one are used to control things like motors. Because transistors are made by modifying just one material, silicon, they can also be formed by the thousand on a single chip.

Connecting leads

MAGNIFIED MICROCHIP
The microchip made electronics into a force that could change the world. The first experimental silicon chip was made in 1958. Early commercial chips contained only a few dozen transistors – now they may contain over a million.

Arm moves to a track to retrieve information stored there

The read/write head is guided by information stored on the disk itself

Track selector mechanism

DISK DRIVE
Memory makes computers useful. Without it, information and instructions would have to be passed to and from the machine by hand, slowing everything to human speed. Computers have fast electronic memories to store whatever is currently being worked on. A slower memory, like this magnetic disk from a personal computer, is better for other data: it is cheaper and does not lose its memory when the power is turned off. When the computer needs something from the disk, it can find it in a fraction of a second.

The hard disk is coated with a magnetic material

COMPUTER SIMULATION

Computers are now a vital tool for all kinds of designers (pp. 52-53). Designers of advanced technology have massive computing power available. Computer workstations – machines many times faster and with much more memory than an ordinary personal computer – can now convert mathematics into pictures like this at astonishing speed. To produce this single image, showing the airflow around a space vehicle re-entering the atmosphere, the workstation had to perform calculations that would have taken an unaided designer most of their working life. Using such a tool, a design can be modified repeatedly until it performs as required.

Drill cuts the plastic

Leading edge of probe shown in simulation

The computer program ensures the design is followed exactly

Computed vortex flow

Color is added electronically back on Earth

Waste material

The three-dimensional image is created by a computer working with digitalized information sent back from the probe

COMPUTER-AIDED DESIGN

Designers used to spend days on drawings and calculations, after which a skilled machinist would cut the design in metal. Now designers can see their work take shape on a computer-controlled cutting machine, which cuts three-dimensional shapes from solid plastic.

Mosaic is incomplete

IO, ONE OF JUPITER'S MOONS

Without electronic computers, the calculations needed for space flights would be impossible, and without electronic imaging and communications there would be no point in sending out probes anyway. On-board computers guide the probe to capture many images as it circles the planet. These are converted into code and then beamed back to Earth by radio. There, more computers enhance the images and assemble them into the final mosaic, giving scientists a grandstand seat in space. This image of Io, a Moon close to Jupiter, was taken by the *Voyager* probe in 1979.

ELECTRONIC NEWS-GATHERING

Electronics means more than computing. It has also changed the way we see the world. Electronic news-gathering began in the 1970s with the development of lightweight television cameras and video recorders. Disturbing images of war, here in Lebanon in the 1980s, now come straight to us.

Volcanoes throw out plumes of sulfurous material

Medical matters

HOWARD FLOREY (1898-1968)
Florey was an Australian pathologist who isolated the first pure antibiotic, penicillin, from mold in 1939. An antibiotic is a substance that kills micro-organisms without harming people.

BEFORE THE GROWTH OF MODERN SCIENCE and medicine, people accepted death and disease as normal. But gradually people came to believe that the body was just a complicated machine, to be mended like any other. Modern technology supports this approach. The technology can be frightening and is sometimes resented, but it is kinder than the brutal methods of 150 years ago. Some of the greatest advances have been in diagnostic machines that help doctors determine what is wrong, and in improved equipment to carry out surgery and keep patients alive while it is going on. Now we can see deep into the body without cutting the skin, operate inside it without leaving an unsightly scar, or even replace entire organs like kidneys or hearts.

ROMAN BONE SAW
Living bone is tough. It takes hard work with a sharp saw to get through it. This 2,000-year-old Roman surgical implement would have been used for cutting through bone in amputations. Operations were carried out without any thought for hygiene.

A wooden handle was attached here

EARLY AMPUTATION
This 18th-century surgeon probably washed his hands only after sawing off the patient's forearm. Even if the patient survived the operation, he might not have survived the bacteria that filled the room. Anesthetics to reduce the pain were not introduced until about 1850, and antiseptics to sterilize the wound later still.

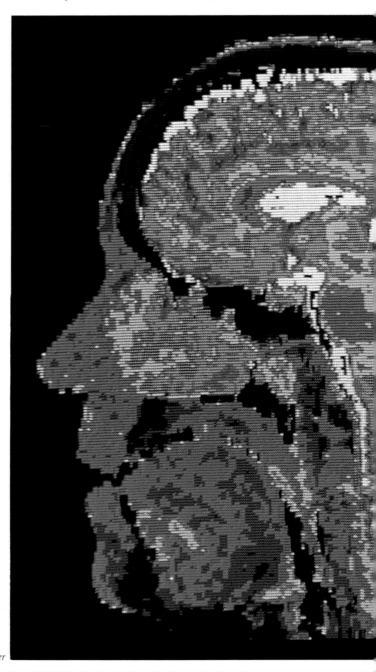

BLOOD-SUCKING LEECH
For centuries, people believed that fevers were caused by too much blood in the body. The obvious cure was to let some out, and the best available technology was the leech, an animal that lives in water and is related to the earthworm. The leech's only food is blood. It bites with tiny teeth and hangs on with suckers while chemicals in its saliva make the blood flow freely. The saliva also contains an anesthetic, so the bite may not be noticed. Doctors stopped using leeches about 60 years ago, but now they are back in favor as a source of chemicals that restore blood flow after surgery and prevent blood from clotting.

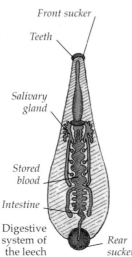

Front sucker

Teeth

Salivary gland

Stored blood

Intestine

Digestive system of the leech

Rear sucker

HOW AN X-RAY WORKS

X-rays were discovered by the German physicist Wilhelm Roentgen (1845-1923) in 1895. They caused a sensation. For the first time, doctors could see right inside the body without even touching it. An X-ray picture (far right) is made by casting shadows onto photographic film. Bones and metal show up clearly because they prevent the rays from getting through. X-rays can also be used to treat cancer.

Television camera

Light from screen

Fluorescent screen

X-rays *The patient*

Electrons fired at target

Target revolves to prevent electrons from overheating it

X-ray tube

QUICK FIX

Broken people can sometimes be fixed almost as quickly as broken cars. Bone is normally a tough natural composite (pp. 28-29), but in older people it can become brittle and then a fall can stress the thigh bone enough to snap the top right off. This X-ray picture shows the result of what is now a routine operation to pin it back on again. A metal such as titanium or stainless steel is used to join the fragments together.

Markings show how far the endoscope has gone in to the body

Tip of endoscope

Tube containing coarse fibers for illumination

Tube containing bundles of fine fibers to form image

Light source attached here

ENDOSCOPY

Surgeons often need a more detailed view inside the body than X-rays or scanners can give. The endoscope apparently defies the laws of optics by bending light around corners to bring out a clear picture. It uses a bundle of glass fibers, each forming a single point of the image.

Steering mechanism

Eyepiece

GODFREY HOUNSFIELD (1919-)

Hounsfield, a British electrical engineer, sent X-rays through the body from many directions on to an electronic detector and then used a computer to picture a slice through the body. He called his method computerized-axial tomography, or "CAT."

IN VITRO FERTILIZATION

Technology can sometimes help childless couples. In suitable cases, a sperm can be injected directly into a human egg, bypassing the normal route. The egg is then put into the woman's womb. If it survives, it will start to grow into a baby.

Sperm injected through hollow needle

Glass tube holds egg steady

A tiny camera on a laparoscope gives a picture that guides a cutting laser to where it is needed

SCANNING THE BRAIN

X-rays are now complemented by images from the nuclear magnetic resonance (NMR) scanner, developed in the late 1970s. It works because atoms in a strong magnetic field wobble around at a rate close to the frequency of a radio wave. By tuning the wave, the atoms can be made to wobble in time with it, absorbing energy. When the wave is turned off, the energy is given out again, allowing the concentration of atoms to be measured. By varying the magnetic field and the radio wave, and putting all the measurements together with a computer, even delicate tissues like the brain can be revealed in some detail. The colors are generated by the computer.

KEYHOLE SURGERY

Often, little actual surgery is required inside the body, but getting at the site of the problem inflicts a lot of damage, causing pain and slowing recovery. Television cameras and lasers now help surgeons operate through small openings, which heal up quickly.

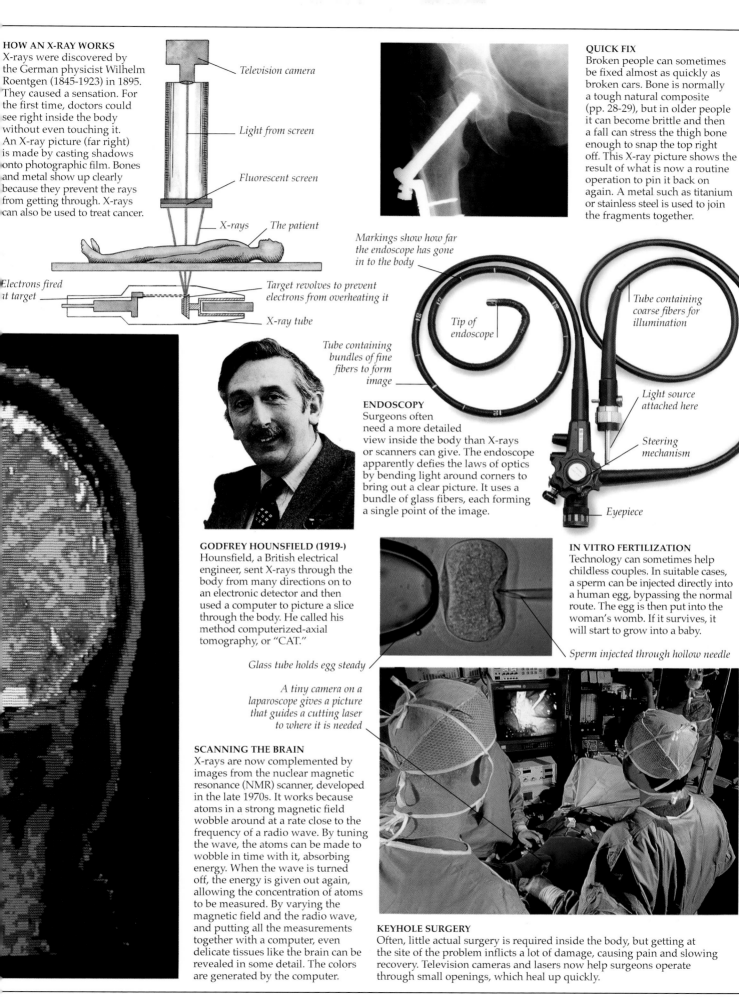

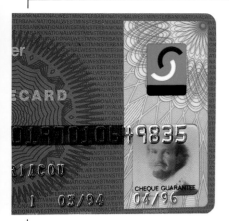

Discovering usefulness

NOT ALL TECHNOLOGY IS A RESPONSE TO NEED. Often, scientists or engineers discover or create things that have no apparent use, but develop them anyway just to see what will happen. The laser came about from ideas first put forward in 1917. It was developed into a working device in 1960, partly to demonstrate that theories about atoms were right. But within ten years this scientific toy had found dozens of practical uses. Some of them, like holograms, were waiting for laser light to make them work. Others, like laser surgery, were totally new. In the 19th century, the discovery of infrared light by British scientist William Herschel (1738-1822) led to a similar story. Infrared light is now an everyday tool, revealing heat loss or, when produced by another sort of laser, picking the music off CDs so it can be heard.

ISAAC NEWTON (1643-1727)
Newton studied light and concluded that it was made of tiny particles shooting through space. This idea fell out of favor, but in the early 20th century particles of light – photons – became the basis of the thinking that led to the laser.

SCIENCE CENTER AT LA VILLETTE, PARIS
Light is made of waves in space. When the waves are other than perfectly regular, an image is seen. A hologram is able to take the regular light waves from a laser and bend them into waves like those that bounced off the original subject – here an architectural model. The three-dimensional image that is seen changes as the viewer moves.

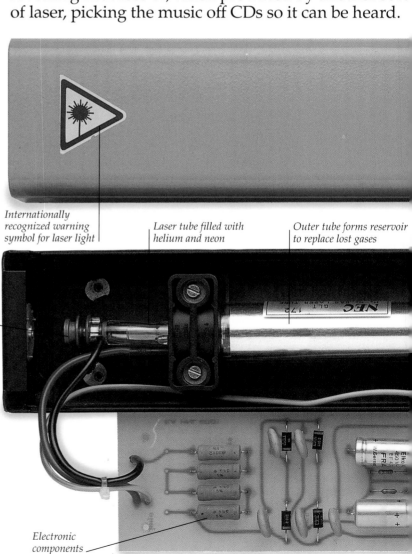

Internationally recognized warning symbol for laser light

Laser tube filled with helium and neon

Outer tube forms reservoir to replace lost gases

Electronic components

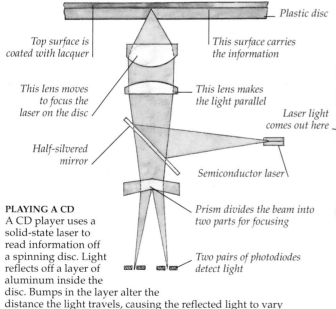

Plastic disc

Top surface is coated with lacquer

This surface carries the information

This lens moves to focus the laser on the disc

This lens makes the light parallel

Laser light comes out here

Half-silvered mirror

Semiconductor laser

PLAYING A CD
A CD player uses a solid-state laser to read information off a spinning disc. Light reflects off a layer of aluminum inside the disc. Bumps in the layer alter the distance the light travels, causing the reflected light to vary in brightness. The light is detected by four photodiodes (light-sensitive electronic devices) and turned into music. The player keeps the laser in focus and on track by adjusting the reading head until each of the photodiodes sees the same amount of light.

Prism divides the beam into two parts for focusing

Two pairs of photodiodes detect light

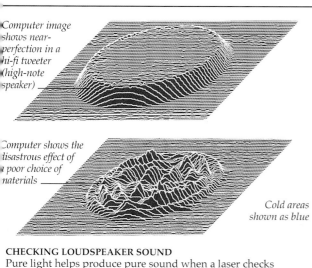

Computer image shows near-perfection in a hi-fi tweeter (high-note speaker)

Computer shows the disastrous effect of a poor choice of materials

CHECKING LOUDSPEAKER SOUND

Pure light helps produce pure sound when a laser checks the performance of a new loudspeaker design. If the speaker produces vibrations of its own, instead of just following the vibrations of the music, it will not reproduce sound realistically. A laser can scan the surface of a working loudspeaker to see if unwanted ripples are present. To do this, the brightness of the laser is varied very rapidly as it sweeps from side to side and up and down to illuminate the moving surface of the speaker. From the way the brightness of the reflected light varies, electronics can then work out how fast and in which direction each point of the surface is moving. Computer printouts of the measurements, as shown here, help the acoustic engineer to see the cause of any problem – in this case a poor choice of materials for the speaker.

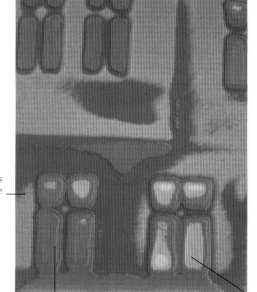

Cold areas shown as blue

Warm areas shown as red

INFRARED HOUSE

Everything gives off a form of radiation similar to light. The radiation from cool things has a wavelength much greater than that of light, and is therefore invisible. As the temperature rises, the wavelength shrinks until eventually a red glow appears – the object has become red-hot. But well before this point is reached, infrared light (infra means "below" in Latin) is being produced. So using a camera that can "see" infrared light is a good way of picturing the temperature of things that are fairly cool. The blue of the walls in this infrared image of a house shows that they are cold, but the red coloration of the windows indicates that they are as warm as the air inside – a sure sign that precious energy is being lost.

Very warm areas shown as yellow

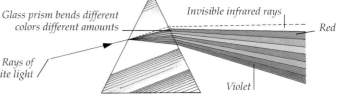

Glass prism bends different colors different amounts

Invisible infrared rays

Red

Rays of white light

Violet

WHAT IS INFRARED LIGHT?

A glass prism produces a spectrum by separating the different waves that make up white light. The spectrum becomes invisible at either end. In 1800 William Herschel, studying sunlight, placed a thermometer just beyond the red part of its spectrum. The temperature rose, showing that invisible energy was falling on it. Herschel called the unseen rays "infrared" light.

LASER EAR SURGERY

The working parts of the ear are buried deep in the skull, protected by solid bone. When something goes wrong, surgeons have to decide whether to operate and risk some damage, or leave the patient intact but with a disability. Technology cannot solve all problems, but this argon laser provides an alternative to the scalpel. High-powered blue light is beamed deep into the ear, where the surgeon, viewing its effect through a microscope, can burn away tumors or reshape tiny bones.

RUBY LASER

The first laser was built by American physicist Theodore Maiman (b. 1927) in 1960. Its light came from a ruby rod. This laser uses a tube containing helium and neon, so is much cheaper. When electricity passes through a gas like neon, its atoms absorb energy, becoming excited. If struck by a photon with the right energy, an excited atom will emit an exactly similar photon. Trapped by mirrors, the photons hit other atoms, making them give out more photons, and so on until a flood of identical photons – laser light – streams out through the half-silvered mirror at one end of the tube.

Technology and nature

TECHNOLOGY HAS USED TINY MICROSCOPIC ORGANISMS for thousands of years. Brewing and baking make use of yeasts, single-celled organisms that can live and multiply in sugary liquids. Bacteria can breed in milk, turning it into cheese. However, modern biotechnology goes well beyond these traditional techniques. Molds are grown to produce antibiotics (p. 56), and can also be harvested as a source of proteins. A most important development has been the understanding of the mechanism of life. It is based on DNA, a unique organic molecule that can reproduce itself and control the production of proteins. Genetic engineering, changing an organism's DNA to make it behave differently, is a challenging new technology that has only just begun.

AN EARLY TECHNOLOGY
Brewing, a way of preserving juices and other sugary extracts from plants, has been practiced for thousands of years. It uses yeasts, microscopic blobs of life that can breed in sugar solutions and turn the sugars into alcohol and the gas carbon dioxide. The gas makes the liquid fizz, while the alcohol eventually kills the yeast, and any other organisms that attempt to grow in the liquid.

NUTRITIOUS MOLD
Most people eat only a limited range of foods. Insects, for example, although nutritious, are not popular as food in most countries. The idea of eating mold also strikes many people as odd, but this tasty product, known as Quorn, can be cooked by conventional methods such as frying and is an excellent source of fat-free protein. It is made by growing molds in large fermenters. After extracting water from the brew, the valuable food that remains is compressed into handy blocks.

MAKING GOAT'S CHEESE
There are hundreds of kinds of cheese (p. 46), produced when the milk of cows, goats, or sheep is attacked by invisible organisms called bacteria. Several sorts of bacteria, some of them harmless relatives of organisms that cause disease, can make cheese. Bacteria feed on the sugar in milk, turning it into acid and causing curd to form (p. 46). Each bacterium gives its own special flavor to the cheese it makes.

Curd from goat's milk is put into "logs"

LOOKING AT GENES
DNA carries the chemical code that passes life from one generation to the next. A section of code that controls a single feature is called a gene. Each gene is made of bases strung together. All living forms are made by arranging the same four bases into different patterns, just as different books are written using the same alphabet. Genes can now be seen as a pattern of lines on a plate. Scientists can then study how different organisms are related by comparing their genes.

Traditional log shapes for goat's cheese

Curd drains before being turned out

Fresh cheese

PROTECTIVE MOLD
Much of the flavor of traditional cheeses also comes from molds. Freshly prepared cheese is open to attack by unwanted bacteria, but under the right conditions mold spores (the mold equivalent of seeds) settle on maturing cheeses and grow, killing bacteria and forming a delicious, protective crust.

The cheese after 7 days with mold crust forming

The mature cheese has an outer layer of mold that protects it

LIFE-SAVING BACTERIA
Insulin is a chemical messenger that controls the storage of sugars in our bodies. It is made by the pancreas, a gland just behind the stomach, and was discovered by Canadian scientists Frederick Banting (1891-1941) and Charles Best (1899-1978) in 1921. People who cannot make enough insulin get too much glucose in their blood after meals, causing damage to the body. Extra insulin solves the problem. It used to come from pigs, but bacteria are now made to produce perfect insulin by splicing human genes into their own DNA. Grown in a fermenter, the unsuspecting bacteria churn out quantities of the vital agent.

In-vitro cultivation

Although genetic engineers can identify genes and move them around, they cannot yet design and make them. It is the natural world that provides the raw material for biotechnology. But as the natural world is being destroyed by other human activities, many organizations are now building up gene banks, where unique plant and animal features can be preserved for use when their wild carriers are extinct. Seeds are an obvious form of gene storage, but living plants are a safer medium. Seeds of threatened orchids can be grown in vitro (Latin for "in glass") and treated almost like test-tube babies (p. 57).

RECOGNIZING THE SEED
Unlike other plants, orchids launch their offspring into the world without a ready-made food supply wrapped up in their seeds. In nature, the tiny embryo orchid inside each seed cannot grow without the help of a particular fungus to provide extra nutrition.
To ensure that the genes of these endangered species survive, techniques that provide or replace the fungus are used. High magnification, here about 1,000 times, helps identify the seeds.

Grains of oatmeal to feed the plant

Growing orchid

Agar enriched with sugars, salts, vitamins, and charcoal

GROWING IN AGAR
When the plants get bigger, they can be transferred to jars. After several more months the orchids are big enough to be put into pots and handled by normal gardening methods. Each of the millions of cells in the mature plant will contain a copy of the original embryo's genes, greatly enhancing the genes' chances of survival.

Electron microscope picture of the cells in the pancreas that produce insulin

The colors are generated electronically

SOWING THE SEED
Dry, sterile seeds are sown on a dish of agar containing ground oats as food. Baby orchids cannot use the food without help, so the right fungus, or an artificial substitute, also goes into the dish. The seeds are kept in the dark until they germinate. If fungus is being used there is a danger that it will kill the tiny plants, so they are soon transferred to a fresh dish. After several months the plants will grow to the size seen here.

A cell that produces another hormone, glucagon

The flowers that produce the dust-fine seeds

A cell in the pancreas that produces insulin

THE FINISHED PLANT
This beautiful blue orchid, *Vanda caerulea*, grows only in tropical countries such as those of southeast Asia, where its continued existence is uncertain. By means of in-vitro cultivation, the almost invisible seed is turned into a handsome plant that lives to carry its unique genetic inheritance into the future.

61

Looking to the future

UNIVERSAL SOLDIER
Science fiction has never recognized limits to change. This scene from the film *Universal Soldier* (1992) anticipates a future in which the human body is merely one component of a machine.

FOR MOST OF HUMAN HISTORY, technology has met simple needs in simple ways. But over the last 200 years, with the emergence of heat engines fueled by coal and oil (pp. 36-37), technology has become a dominant force. For many people, new machines and methods have brought happiness and fulfillment. Others have seen their settled way of life destroyed. In the future, technology may not be able to maintain its present rate of development, with its destructive effect on the natural world and its dependence on energy from fuels that cannot be replaced. Governments are beginning to talk about the problem, while engineers and scientists are working on cleaner, safer technologies. Research into new energy sources now has a higher priority, recycling of many materials is routine, and more appropriate technologies are being found for poorer countries. All these things can help, although ordinary people may need to change their expectations. Our unique ability to bend the world to our will could make life worse, not better.

Shaft and blades molded in one piece

CERAMIC TURBOCHARGER
This is part of a turbocharger from a car, a device that makes the engine more powerful. The new component is made of ceramic, one of our oldest materials (p. 8). Efforts are being made to reduce the brittleness of ceramics so that they can be used to make more efficient car engines.

Curved blades turned by hot exhaust gases

Recycling materials

Extracting metals takes energy. Paper comes from trees, which grow slowly. Water comes from a fixed supply of rain. Plastics and fuels come from oil, which cannot be replaced. By recycling, these materials can be used without putting too much strain on natural resources. Getting aluminum from used cans, for instance, takes far less energy than extracting it from its ore. Many new products are now made from recycled materials.

SLUDGE PONDS
People make waste, and waste pollutes unless it is dealt with properly. This activated-sludge plant uses air bubbles to speed up the natural breakdown of human waste by microorganisms. Bacteria added to the waste consume the unwanted solids leaving a scum that settles to the bottom. The remaining water can then be safely returned to a river.

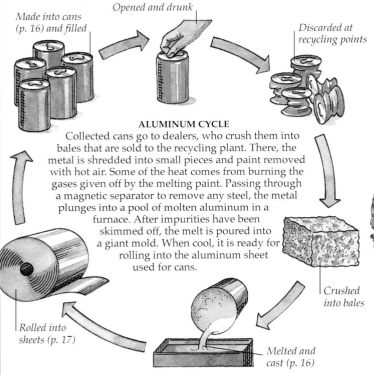

Made into cans (p. 16) and filled

Opened and drunk

Discarded at recycling points

ALUMINUM CYCLE
Collected cans go to dealers, who crush them into bales that are sold to the recycling plant. There, the metal is shredded into small pieces and paint removed with hot air. Some of the heat comes from burning the gases given off by the melting paint. Passing through a magnetic separator to remove any steel, the metal plunges into a pool of molten aluminum in a furnace. After impurities have been skimmed off, the melt is poured into a giant mold. When cool, it is ready for rolling into the aluminum sheet used for cans.

Crushed into bales

Rolled into sheets (p. 17)

Melted and cast (p. 16)

CONVENIENT COLLECTION
The problem with recycling consumer products like cans, clothes, or newspapers is that it takes energy to gather products together once they have been distributed. A can bank is of little value if people have to drive a long way to deliver just a few cans: they may use more fuel than it would take to make the cans from raw materials. The secret of recycling is to allow consumers to dump products at a central point in the course of routines like shopping, so that they do not have to use extra fuel. Each of these bales contains thousands of cans collected in this way.

HARVESTING THE WIND

Our only inexhaustible source of energy is the Sun. By heating the atmosphere unevenly and creating differences of air pressure, some of the Sun's energy ends up as the energy of moving air. Wind farms can turn this into electrical energy. The turbines on this wind farm are modern versions of the windmills that were used for centuries before electricity was thought of. Wind power does not cause any chemical pollution, but the turbines can be noisy and they change the look of the landscape. It takes a large area of wind farm to generate a small amount of electricity. If all the suitable sites in the US were used, they would generate only about 10 percent of current demand. One answer to this problem is for people to waste less energy.

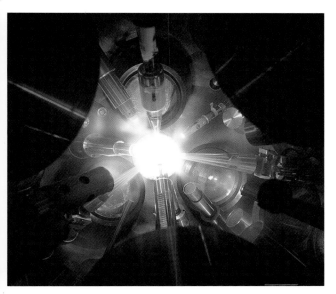

ENERGY FROM HYDROGEN

Scientists have been trying for years to control the energy of the hydrogen bomb. If this could be done, nearly limitless energy would be available from water, which contains the necessary kinds of "heavy" hydrogen atoms, deuterium and tritium. Here, a frozen pellet of these materials is being blasted with two billion kilowatts of laser power, heating it instantly to 100 million °C, in the hope of making the atomic nuclei fuse and release energy for human consumption.

MAKING A WATER PUMP

It is easy for to forget that huge numbers of people do not have refrigerators, telephones, or computer games. Many people have been forced to make maximum use of scarce energy and materials in a way that could become normal in the future. Toys, for instance, are not made from expensive plastics. They are made instead from odds and ends of scrap materials, but are no less fun to play with. This toy pump is made from an old oil can, wood, string, a leftover pipe, and some spare fencing wire. It works just like the real thing: a type of pump that is simple to make, uses only human energy, and is widely used for irrigation in less-developed countries.

Log carved into pulley

Oil can receives water

String with rubber washers attached at regular intervals

Turning the handle pulls the washers up the pipe, bringing water with them

String holds parts together

Fencing wire frame

Clay seal

Outlet pipe takes water to where it is needed

Plastic pipe

Index

Acknowledgments

Dorling Kindersley would like to thank the following organizations and individuals:
Lexus (GB) Ltd; Pantone, Inc., 590 Commerce Blvd., Carlstadt, NJ 07072-3098 USA. PANTONE® is the registered trademark of Pantone, Inc.; The Ironbridge Gorge Museum Trust; Charlie Westhead at Neals Yard Creamery; Phil Hill and Terry Bennett at Readyweld Plastics Ltd; Brian Patrick and Andrew Rastall at Rolls-Royce plc, Derby; Peter Dickinson and Catherine Smith at Kristol Limited, Stalybridge, Cheshire; Alcan International; Dynamic-Ceramics; Julian Wright at Celestion International Ltd; John Tawn from Deplynn Engineering for the site welding; Peter Griffiths for making the models; Jack Challoner for advice; Frances Halpin for assistance with the materials; Neville Graham, Natalie Hennequin,

and Gary Madison for helping with the design of the book; Anthony Wilson for reading the text; Douglas Garland at R.B.R. Armour Ltd; Dr. Michael Fay at Kew Gardens; Fran Riccini at the Science Museum, Wroughton; Peter Skilton at the Kirkaldy Testing Museum, Southwark; Naine Woodrow and Tom Hughes from the North Street Potters, London SW4.

Illustrations John Woodcock, Janos Marffy, Nick Hall, Philip Argent, and Eugene Fleury
Photography Peter Anderson, Peter Chadwick, Andy Crawford, Philip Dowell, David Exton, Philip Gatward, Christi Graham, Peter Hayman, Chas Howson, Colin Keates, Dave King, David Murray, Mike Nicholls, Tim Ridley, Susanna Price.
Index Jane Parker

Picture credits
t=top b=bottom c=center l=left r=right
Alcan International 14l, 14b, 62br. All Sport 7tl. Arcaid 53tr. British Library 50 tl. British Museum 8tl, 12tr, 14tl, 24c. Bruce Coleman 61br. e.t. Archive 34cr, 35bl, 44tl, 44brt. Mary Evans Picture Library 34tr, 39cl, 47tl, 53tc. Ronald Grant Archive 62tl. Robert Harding Picture Library 7tr, 9tr, 10bl, 11c, 17tr, 24cl. Hulton Deutsch 29tl, 34bl, 42cl, 53tl, 56c. Illustrated London News 40cl. Image Select 6cl, 36tl, 44bl, 46tr. Mansell Collection 16cl, 38tl, 58tr. Microscopix 18tl. M.I.R.A. 43tr, 53cl. NASA 55br. Richard Olivier 49br. Robert Opie Collection 39c. Popperphoto cover, 37br, 39bl, 57cl. Q.A. Photos 21tr. Range/Bettmann 46cr. Rex Features 8tl, 43cr, 44tr, 55bl. Rolls-Royce plc Derby 3bl, 4br, 7bl, 15bl, 15cl, 15cr, 53c, 53b, 53c, 53bl. Scala 21tl, 34br. Science Photo Library 7br, 13tr,/Astrid and Hans Frieder Micheler 14tc & 15tc,/Ben Johnson 16cr,/Dr Jeremy Burgess 27br,/Simon Fraser 31tl,/Philippe Plailly 35br,/George Haling 43c,/James King Holmes 47cl,/Geoff Lane 47bl,/Malcom Feilding 54tl,

/John Walsh 54cr,/Ross Ressemeyer 55tr, 56tl,/Martin Dohru 56bl, 56-57, 57tr,/Hank Morgan 57c,/Geoff Tompkinson 57br,/Phillippe Plailly 58cl,/Alexander Tsiaras 59br,/James King Holmes 6ocr,/Sechi-Lecaque 61bl,/John Walsh 62c,/Hank Morgan 62cr,/Roger Rossemeyer 63tl,/Martin Bond 63tl. Zefa cover c, 17br, 21c, 37tl, 44bl, 51br, 55cl, 59tc.

The objects on these pages are in the collections of the following museums: University of Archaeology and Anthropology, Cambridge 14tl. British Museum 8tl, 12tl, 12cl, 16tl, 24cr, 35l, 39tr, 56cl. Design Museum, London 29tr, 32/33c, 40r, 41tl, 43tl, 49cl, 52b, 52cl. Ironbridge Gorge Museum, Shropshire 12cr, 13tl, 13cl, 13cr, 16b, 17b. Kew Gardens, London 61tl, 61c, 61cr. Kirkaldy Testing Museum, London 12br, 13bl, 20b, 21b. Museum of London 12tl. Natural History Museum, London 10tl, 26tl. Pitt Rivers Museum, Oxford 12bl. Science Museum, London 9bc, 9cr, 9bl, 22/23b, 27cr, 27cl, 28/29cb, 29cl, 30t, 30c, 30b, 31c, 32lc, 34c, 35tr, 40bc, 41c, 42/43b, 44c, 45cl, 47tr, 47tcr, 54cl, 54c, 57cr.